T h e

Newbery

a n d

Caldecott

Awards

▶ A Guide
to the
Medal
a n d
Honor
Books

2007
Edition

Association for
Library Service to Children

AMERICAN LIBRARY ASSOCIATION

Chicago   2007

Photo of Susan Patron used with permission of Simon & Schuster, Inc. Cover illustration for *The Higher Power of Lucky,* by Susan Patron, illustrated by Matt Phelan, copyright © 2006, used with permission of Richard Jackson Books/Atheneum Books for Young Readers, an imprint of Simon & Schuster Children's Division.

Photo of David Wiesner © Peggy Morsch. Cover illustration for *Flotsam,* by David Wiesner, used with permission of Clarion Books.

The paper used in this publication meets the minimum requirements of American National Standard for Information Sciences—Permanence of Paper for Printed Library Materials, ANSI Z39.48-1992.♾

ISBN-10: 0-8389-3567-2
ISBN-13: 978-0-8389-3567-5
ISSN: 1070-4493

Printed in the United States of America

11 10 09 08 07   5 4 3 2 1

CONTENTS

PREFACE

Welcome to the 2007 edition of the Newbery and Caldecott awards guide. This complete listing of Newbery and Caldecott Medal–winning titles and Honor Books showcases the most distinguished examples of American children's literature over the past eighty-plus years. There is quite a bit of history here!

The Newbery and Caldecott Awards is reissued each year, featuring the new medal and honor books and listing the previous awards from their inceptions in 1922 (Newbery Medal) and 1938 (Caldecott Medal). In this year's essay, Barbara Elleman presents an exciting account of the origin and early history of the Newbery Medal. It's fascinating to look at the early winners through a contemporary lens; it's hard to imagine some of the winning books being so honored today, but it's gratifying to see how many of these classics remain relevant.

Bette J. Peltola's essay "Newbery and Caldecott Awards: Authorization and Terms" discusses the terms and definitions that have evolved for both awards. She provides insight into the significance of the awards and into the evaluation of children's literature.

We have included photos of the 2007 Newbery and Caldecott medalists and the remarks of the award committee chairs, which provide some insight into why these books were selected. "The Media Used in Caldecott Picture Books" reveals each illustrator's choice of media for the Caldecott Medal–winning books and Honor Books (1938–2007) and includes a helpful glossary of art terms.

We hope you will find the 2007 guide valuable, and we welcome your suggestions for future editions.

DIANE FOOTE
Executive Director
Association for Library Service to Children

Newbery and Caldecott Awards
Authorization and Terms

BETTE J. PELTOLA

Each year the Newbery and Caldecott Medals are awarded by the American Library Association for the most distinguished American children's books published the previous year. On June 21, 1921, Frederic G. Melcher proposed to the American Library Association meeting of the Children's Librarians' Section that a medal be given for the most distinguished children's book of the year. He suggested that it be named for the eighteenth-century English bookseller John Newbery. The idea was enthusiastically accepted by the children's librarians, and Melcher's official proposal was approved by the ALA Executive Board in 1922. In Melcher's formal agreement with the board, the purpose of the Newbery Medal was stated as follows: "To encourage original and creative work in the field of books for children. To emphasize to the public that contributions to the literature for children deserve similar recognition to poetry, plays, or novels. To give those librarians, who make it their life work to serve children's reading interests, an opportunity to encourage good writing in this field." The Newbery Award thus became the first children's book award in the world. Its terms, as well as its long history, continue to make it the best known and most discussed children's book award in this country.

The description of the award adopted in 1922 indicated that the Newbery Medal "is to be awarded annually to the author of the 'most distinguished contribution to American literature for children,' the award being made to cover books whose publication in book form falls in the calendar year last elapsed. The award is restricted to authors who are citizens or residents of the United States. Reprints and compilations

BETTE J. PELTOLA is professor emerita, School of Education, University of Wisconsin–Milwaukee.

are not eligible for consideration. There are no limitations as to the character of the book considered except that it be original work. It need not be written solely for children; the judgment of the librarians voting shall decide whether a book be a 'contribution to the literature for children.' The award considers only the books of one calendar year and does not pass judgment on the author's previous work or other work during that year outside the volume that may be named." In 1932 the Section for Library Work with Children, with Melcher's approval, adopted the following: "To be eligible for the Newbery Medal books must be original, or, if traditional in origin, the result of individual research, the retelling and reinterpretation being the writer's own."

During the next several years, many persons became concerned that the artists creating picture books for children were as deserving of honor and encouragement as were the authors of children's books. So, in 1937 Melcher suggested a second annual medal, this to be given to the artist who had created the most distinguished picture book of the year and to be called the Caldecott Medal in honor of Randolph Caldecott, the nineteenth-century English illustrator. The idea for this medal was also accepted enthusiastically by the Section for Library Work with Children of ALA and was approved by the ALA Executive Board.

The Caldecott Medal "shall be awarded to the artist of the most distinguished American Picture Book for Children published in the United States during the preceding year. The award shall go to the artist, who must be a citizen or resident of the United States, whether or not he be the author of the text. Members of the Newbery Medal Committee will serve as judges. If a book of the year is nominated for both the Newbery and Caldecott Awards the committee shall decide under which heading it shall be voted upon, so that the same title shall not be considered on both ballots." In 1977 the Board of Directors of the Association for Library Service to Children rescinded the final part of the 1937 action and approved that "any book published in the preceding year shall be eligible to be considered for either award or both awards." Separate committees to choose the Newbery and Caldecott Awards were established in 1978 and began with the 1980 Selection Committees.

ADDITIONAL CHANGES IN TERMS FOR THE AWARDS

A resolution by the Section for Library Work with Children in 1932 that "the book of a previous award winner shall receive the award only upon the unanimous vote" of the committee was later rescinded by the Children's Services Division Board of Directors. "In view of the fact that a unanimous vote in the case of a previous winner of the Newbery or Caldecott Awards was first instituted to encourage new authors and illustrators at a period when such encouragement was needed and since such need is no longer apparent, the restriction of a unanimous vote for winning either award more than once [is] removed from terms for selection [of the awards]" (1958). In 1963 it was voted by the Children's Services Division that "joint authors shall be eligible" for the awards.

In 1978, the ALSC Board of Directors adopted new statements of terms, definitions, and criteria for each award. The new statements were prepared and adopted to provide further clarification of the basis on which the awards are to be given. They were slightly modified for further clarification in 1985 and 1987.

NEWBERY AWARD

The terms, definitions, and criteria for the Newbery Award are as follows:

TERMS

1. The Medal shall be awarded annually to the author of the most distinguished contribution to American literature for children published in the United States during the preceding year. There are no limitations as to the character of the book considered except that it be original work. Honor Books may be named. These shall be books that are also truly distinguished.

2. The Award is restricted to authors who are citizens or residents of the United States.

3. The committee in its deliberations is to consider only the books eligible for the Award as specified in the terms.

DEFINITIONS

1. "*Contribution* to American *literature*" indicates the text of a book. It also implies that the committee shall consider all forms of writing—fiction, nonfiction, and poetry. Reprints and compilations are not eligible.

2. A "Contribution to American literature for *children*" shall be a book for which children are a potential audience. The book displays respect for children's understandings, abilities, and appreciations. "Children" are defined as persons of ages up to and including fourteen, and books for this entire age range are to be considered.

3. "Distinguished" is defined as:
   • marked by eminence and distinction: noted for significant achievement
   • marked by excellence in quality
   • marked by conspicuous excellence or eminence
   • individually distinct

4. "Author" may include coauthors. The author may be awarded the medal posthumously.

5. In defining the term "original work," the committee will consider books that are traditional in origin if the book is the result of original research and the retelling and interpretation are the writer's own.

6. "American literature published in the United States" means that books originally published in other countries are not eligible.

7. "Published . . . during the preceding year" means that the book has a publication date in that year, was available for purchase in that year, and has a copyright date no later than that year. A book might have a copyright date prior to the year under consideration but, for various reasons, was not published until the year under consideration.

8. "Resident" specifies that the author has established and maintained residence in the United States as distinct from being a casual or occasional visitor.

9. The term "only the books eligible for the Award" specifies that the committee is not to consider the entire body of the work of an author or whether the author has previously won the award. The committee's decision is to be made following deliberations about the books of the specified calendar year.

CRITERIA

1. In identifying distinguished writing in a book for children:
   a. Committee members need to consider:
      Interpretation of the theme or concept.

      Presentation of information including accuracy, clarity, and organization.

      Development of plot.

      Delineation of characters.

      Delineation of setting.

      Appropriateness of style.

   Note: Because the literary qualities to be considered will vary depending on content, the committee need not expect to find excellence in each of the named elements. The book should, however, have distinguished qualities in all of the elements pertinent to it.

   b. Committee members must consider excellence of presentation for a child audience.

2. Each book is to be considered as a contribution to literature. The committee is to make its decision primarily on the text. Other aspects of a book are to be considered only if they distract from the text. Such other aspects might include illustrations, overall design of the book, etc.

   Note: The committee should keep in mind that the award is for literary quality and quality of presentation for children. The award is not for didactic intent or for popularity.

CALDECOTT AWARD

The terms, definitions, and criteria for the Caldecott Award are as follows:

TERMS

1. The Medal shall be awarded annually to the artist of the most distinguished American picture book for children published in the United States during the preceding year. There are no limitations as to the character of the picture book except that the illustrations be original work. Honor Books may be named. These shall be books that are also truly distinguished.

2. The Award is restricted to artists who are citizens or residents of the United States.

3. The committee in its deliberations is to consider only the books eligible for the Award, as specified in the terms.

DEFINITIONS

1. A "picture book for children," as distinguished from other books with illustrations, is one that essentially provides the child with a visual experience. A picture book has a collective unity of story line, theme, or concept, developed through the series of pictures of which the book is comprised.

2. A "picture book for children" is one for which children are a potential audience. The book displays respect for children's understandings, abilities, and appreciations. "Children" are defined as persons of ages up to and including fourteen, and picture books for this entire age range are to be considered.

3. "Distinguished" is defined as:
   - marked by eminence and distinction: noted for significant achievement
   - marked by excellence in quality
   - marked by conspicuous excellence or eminence
   - individually distinct

4. The "artist" is the illustrator or co-illustrators. The artist may be awarded the medal posthumously.

5. "Original work" means that illustrations reprinted or compiled from other sources are not eligible.

6. "American picture book published in the United States" specifies that books originally published in other countries are not eligible.

7. "Published . . . in the preceding year" means that the book has a publication date in that year, was available for purchase in that year, and has a copyright date no later than that year. A book might have a copyright date prior to the year under consideration but, for various reasons, was not published until the year under consideration.

8. "Resident" specifies that the artist has established and maintained residence in the United States as distinct from being a casual or occasional visitor.

9. The term "only the books eligible for the Award" specifies that the committee is not to consider the entire body of the work by an artist or whether the artist has previously won the award. The committee's decision is to be made following deliberation about the picture books of the specified calendar year.

CRITERIA

1. In identifying a distinguished picture book for children:

    a. Committee members need to consider:

      Excellence of execution in the artistic technique employed.

      Excellence of pictorial interpretation of story, theme, or concept; of appropriateness of style of illustration to the story, theme, or concept; of delineation of plot, theme, characters, setting, mood, or information through the pictures.

    b. Committee members must consider excellence of presentation in recognition of a child audience.

2. The only limitation to graphic form is that the form must be one which may be used in a picture book (e.g., motion-picture photography is not at present possible, though still photography is).

3. Each book is to be considered as a picture book. The committee is to make its decision primarily on the illustrations, but other components of a book are to be considered especially when they make a book less effective as a children's picture book. Such other components might include the written text, the overall design of the book, and so forth.

    Note: The committee should keep in mind that the award is for distinguished illustrations in a picture book and for excellence of pictorial presentation for children. The award is not for didactic intent or for popularity.

AWARD COMMITTEES

The committees that select the Newbery and the Caldecott Medal and Honor Books each have fifteen members including the chair. The ALSC membership elects the chair and seven members from a slate drawn up by the nominating committee; the ALSC president-elect appoints the remaining seven members. All members of the committees are members of ALSC.

During the year, each committee member reads as many of the eligible books as possible, including all books suggested by other committee members and by other members of ALSC. Twice in the autumn, committee members cast preliminary ballots to begin to focus attention on the books likely to be of most interest in the selection discussions. No eligible book which has been suggested before the midwinter selection meetings is excluded from consideration, however, even if it was not nominated on a preliminary ballot. During the selection meetings, the committee discusses all nominated and suggested books before beginning balloting. Each committee member votes for three books, with four points assigned to first choice, three to second, and two to third choice. To win, a book must receive at least eight first place choices and at least eight points more than any other book. Once a winner is chosen, the committee decides whether to name honor books and how many.

DESCRIPTION OF THE MEDALS

In 1921 Melcher had the Newbery Medal designed by Rene Paul Chambellan. In 1937 Chambellan designed the Caldecott Medal. The bronze medals, shown on page 8, have the winner's name and the date engraved on the back. The ALA Executive Board in 1922 delegated to the Children's Librarians' Section the responsibility for selecting the book to receive the Newbery Medal. The inscription on the Newbery Medal still reads "Children's Librarians' Section," although the section has changed its name four times and its membership now includes both school and public library children's librarians in contrast to the years 1922–58, when the section, under three different names, included only public library children's librarians. (The section names: until 1929, Children's Librarians' Section; 1929–42, Section for Library Work with Children; 1942–58, Children's Library Association; 1958–77, Children's Service Division; and, Association for Library Service to Children [ALSC], 1977 to date.)

When the Caldecott Medal was accepted in 1937, the Section for Library Work with Children invited the School Libraries Section (now American Association of School Librarians) to name five of its members to the awards committee each year. For this reason the Caldecott Medal inscription reads: "Awarded annually by the Children's and School Librarians Sections of the American Library Association." This is a combination and simplification of the actual names of the sections. The wording continues even though several ALA reorganizations resulted in 1958 in the present divisions, among them the Children's Services Division (now the Association for Library Service to Children), made up of public library children's librarians, school librarians, and others interested in children's library services and good books for children. In 1958 the Children's Services Division Board of Directors recognized that the wording on both medals was incorrect in terms of current ALA terminology. It realized that confusion about the membership of the committee that chooses the medal winners could result from the discrepancies. However, the CSD board decided to request no change in the inscription on either medal, preferring to have them continue in their original form and design. Responsibility for both awards resides with ALSC, formerly the CSD.

HONOR BOOKS

From the beginning of the awarding of the medals, committees could, and usually did, cite other books as worthy of attention. Such books were referred to as runners-up. In 1971 the term "runners-up," used to designate books cited with the annual Newbery and Caldecott Medal winners, was changed to "honor books." The new terminology was made retroactive so that all runners-up are now referred to as Newbery or Caldecott Honor Books.

At the same meeting, the Board of Directors of the Children's Services Division approved silver facsimile seals with the designation "Newbery Honor Book" and "Caldecott Honor Book," which may be placed on the honor books in similar fashion to the use made of the gold facsimile seals of the medals placed on the award-winning books. The gold and silver facsimile seals are sold by the Association for Library Service to Children, with all profits going to support the division's programs, including the Frederic G. Melcher Scholarship Fund. Permission for photographic reproduction of the medals is also controlled by the association; profits from commercial reproduction also go to the Scholarship Fund.

In 1978 the ALSC board approved the presentation of certificates to the authors of the Newbery Honor Books and the illustrators of the Caldecott Honor Books. Certificates were presented for the first time in 1986.

Although some procedures have changed over the years the awards have been given, and some rules or aspects of what the awards are for have been clarified or modified, the basic purpose of honoring distinguished American children's books has not changed. Numerous committees have studied virtually every aspect of the award-giving procedure, the rationale, and the impact of the awards over the years. Such study is likely to continue and ensures a vital life to these awards that have had such an impact on the quality of American literature for children.

JOHN NEWBERY MEDAL	THE CALDECOTT MEDAL

The John Newbery Medal
The First Decade

BARBARA ELLEMAN

June 22, 1921, stands as a monumental date in the history of children's literature: it marks the establishment of the John Newbery Medal for distinguished writing in a book for children. The occasion was the American Library Association's conference in Swampscott, Massachusetts, where more than three hundred children's librarians (a record number) gathered in that seaside community. This unexpectedly large attendance necessitated that the Children's Librarians' Section (as it was then called) crowd into an unused garage behind the New Ocean House hotel. Their two-day opening session featured a panel of librarians detailing the third successful year of Children's Book Week. The next morning, excitement about the growing interest in children's librarianship still permeated the air, but nothing suggested anything revolutionary was about to be put in place.

The agenda for the second session on June 22, presided over by chair Alice Hazeltine of the St. Louis Public Library, was routine: various papers on manufacturing costs of books and other pertinent topics were followed by the annual installation of new officers. Then, at the meeting's close, Frederick Melcher, editor of *Publisher's Weekly*, stepped forward and presented a groundbreaking idea.

Melcher was not a librarian, but as a longtime bookseller and recent publisher he felt a kinship with the library world—especially the world of children's books.

BARBARA ELLEMAN is the founding editor of *Book Links* and served as a children's book editor for *Booklist* and as Distinguished Scholar of Children's Literature at Marquette University. She is the author of *Tomie de Paola: His Art and His Stories* (Putnam, 1999) and *Virginia Lee Burton: A Life in Art* (Houghton, 2002). Now living in Massachusetts, she serves on the Board of Directors at the Eric Carle Museum of Picture Book Art and is advisor to the Barbara Elleman Research Library housed at the Carle Museum.

He had been the instigator of the recently launched Children's Book Week and had spoken eloquently about the project on the previous day, emphasizing the "power [librarians] could have in encouraging the joy of reading among children" (Smith 1957). He seemed to understand innately all aspects of the children's book world and sensed the rising vitality in the growing field of children's literature. In this he was certainly right.

In 1916, Bertha Mahony had opened her highly successful Bookshop for Boys and Girls in Boston; 1918 found Anne Carroll Moore, superintendent of work with children at the New York Public Library, offering critical reviews of children's books in *The Bookman;* 1919, the first year of Children's Book Week, also saw Macmillan appointing the first-ever children's book editor—Louise Seaman. Three years later, Scribner and Doubleday, Page followed suit, choosing Alice Dalgliesh and May Massee, respectively, to head their children's book departments. These three women were the pioneers of what has developed into a distinct—and flourishing—arena of book publishing.

Interest in elevating children's literature was growing in other venues as well. Special rooms for young readers were being established within public libraries across the country; colleges and universities had begun offering courses to train librarians in the art of bringing children and books together; and the media was starting to find children's books worthy of notice.

On June 22, 1921, however, Melcher reached for an even greater role for librarians. He felt strongly that they should not just be caretakers of children's literary heritage but should be encouraging the creative aspects of bookmaking. He feared the conference-generated enthusiasm would melt away when the participants returned to their own communities.

From the bevy of ideas that had been racing through Melcher's mind, one caught hold and crystallized: a medal, to be given annually, for an outstanding children's book. The Pulitzer Prize might ignore the genre, but a competition of literature for the young, he thought, could light a needed fire. It was his hope that such a prize would entice already proven writers and artists to the children's book field.

Caught up in the ebullient mood, the librarians welcomed the idea and voted to put Melcher's idea into effect the very next year. And so it was that the John Newbery Medal "for the most distinguished contribution to American literature for children" came into being.

Looking back, it seems a daring undertaking: the Children's Librarians' Section had only twenty-seven members and $1.95 in its treasury. Today we can only applaud their willingness and energy to take on an undoubtedly daunting task, which, over the years, has turned into an event with far-reaching prestigious and financial implications.

Although in the twenty-first century some find it puzzling that such a coveted American prize would be named after an Englishman, it seemed a natural choice to Melcher and the librarians involved with creating the award. Coincidentally, Melcher had been reading Charles Knight's *Shadows of Old Booksellers* and had been impressed with the lively description of the eighteenth-century bookseller and printer John Newbery. What better way, the publisher thought, to honor the first person to see possibilities in producing books particularly for children. Melcher was later to say that the idea for the award and its name rushed to his mind simultaneously.

A committee of three was immediately organized to head up this new endeavor: Clara W. Hunt, Brooklyn Public Library (named chair); E. Gertrude Avey, Cincinnati Public Library; and Leonore St. John Power, New York Public Library. In the months that followed, the trio wrestled with considerations such as who was entitled to vote, how the final decision would be made, and how to involve librarians nationwide. Concerned that the vote might be close, they decided that a jury, made up of the Children's Librarians' Section officers and four member librarians, would make the final decision.

To publicize both the voting and the presentation of the award, letters asking for nominations for the most distinguished children's book published in 1921 went out to nearly five hundred practicing children's librarians, and notices were published in *Library Journal* and other professional magazines. Nominations were due on March 1, 1922, and all librarians, not just those serving children, were invited to take part. The widespread notice served two other intertwining strategies: to entice librarians to join the slow-growing Children's Librarians' Section and to draw them to the ALA conference for the granting of the first John Newbery Medal.

While Melcher was adamant from the beginning that the Newbery Award belonged in the hands of the American Library Association, he did provide continued guidance and support. He volunteered to find (and pay) someone to create the medal, choosing Rene Paul Chambellan, a young designer who had distinguished himself with a number of large sculptures in New York City. Melcher gave the artist a free hand, his only suggestion being that the medal should reflect "genius giving its best to the child" (Smith 1957).

By March 8, 1922, 212 votes had been received and tabulated. The verdict was unmistakable: Hendrik Willem van Loon, with 163 votes for *The Story of Mankind* (Boni & Liveright, 1921), was named the first Newbery Medal winner. The five other authors who received votes were named "Runners-Up," a designation that was later changed, retroactively, to "Honor Book." They were Charles Boardman Hawes for *The Great Quest* (Little, Brown, 1921) with 22 votes, Bernard Gay Marshall for *Cedric the Forester* (Appleton, 1921) with 7 votes, William Bowen for *The Old Tobacco Shop: A True Account of What Befell a Little Boy in Search of Adventure* (Macmillan, 1921) with 5 votes, Padraic Colum for *The Golden Fleece and the Heroes Who Lived before Achilles* (Macmillan, 1921) with 4 votes, and Cornelia Meigs for *The Windy Hill* (Macmillan, 1921) with 2 votes.

Of these five, Hawes and Meigs would win future Newbery Medals and Meigs would receive three more Honor Book designations in her career. Colum would garner two other Honor Book designations, but Marshall and Bowen left no further mark on the field. While *The Story of Mankind* has stayed in print, none of van Loon's other titles made its way onto a Newbery list. Interestingly, of the four medal-winning publishers (Liveright; Macmillan; Little, Brown; and Appleton) only one—Little, Brown—is still publishing children's books today.

While voting is heavily veiled in today's Newbery Award selection process, such secrecy was obviously not an issue in 1922: the statistics appear in Irene Smith's *A History of the Newbery and Caldecott Medals.* Neither, evidently, was conflict of interest: Leonore St. John Power, a member of the organizing committee, provided a reading list that was included in the first edition of *The Story of Mankind.*

Van Loon was an interesting choice for the first award. Born in Holland in 1892, he immigrated to America in 1902, where he became a well-known journalist, lecturer, college professor, writer, illustrator, and correspondent for NBC. In 1919, he applied for and received American citizenship, just three years before winning the Newbery. He was known to be a womanizer and was married four times, twice to the same woman. His first wife was Eliza Bowditch, great-granddaughter of Nathaniel Bowditch (in 1956 Jean Latham would win a Newbery Medal for a biography of the famous navigator). Widely recognized as an engaging writer, lively public lecturer, and enthusiastic radio commentator, van Loon was often in the news—sometimes shown in a negative light. The *New York Times* once stated, "When Hendrik Willem van Loon writes history, you can be certain of getting both plenty of history and plenty of van Loon" (Unitarian Universalist Historical Society website). While some accused van Loon of sloppy scholarship and of manufacturing details to support his narrative, others championed his flamboyant style.

The Story of Mankind received lavish praise upon its release. Anne Carroll Moore, a powerful influence in the children's book field, heralded the book as "the most invigorating and, I venture to predict, the most influential children's book for many years to come" (Miller and Field 1955). But van Loon's book was not without its detractors. For example, his extended treatment of evolution without mention of the Biblical account of creation deterred a number of libraries from acquiring the book. Nevertheless, *The Story of Mankind* was lauded for "its originality, its boldness of conception, its vigor of phrase and metaphor, and [for] its animated illustrations" (Miller and Field 1955), and this, along with the high proportion of votes it garnered, brought assurance to the Children's Librarians' Section that the first Newbery Medal winner had been chosen well.

Measured by today's standards, van Loon's style seems overblown and somewhat sentimental, but in the 1920s his lively storytelling broke barriers in making history come alive on the page. In 1951, his son Gerard van Loon supplemented his father's work, continuing the story through the First and Second World Wars and into the postwar years; the book was revised again in 1973. The 2005 edition ends with a section called "The Last Fifty Years, Including Several Explanations and an Apology," undoubtedly to appease those concerned with the now-unacceptable cultural and racial slurs in the original edition. It is significant that an informational book won the first Newbery Medal. While nonfiction books have captured Newbery Honors, other than biographies and poetry none has ever won a medal.

ALA held its 1922 conference in Detroit. The meeting of the Children's Librarians' Section, on Tuesday, June 27, devoted time to several papers on the general subject of the book, but the highlight of the afternoon, without a doubt, was the Newbery presentation ceremony.

Eager to build anticipation about the award, Melcher had cautioned the committee to keep the winner's name a secret until the award was presented. Melcher, who had accompanied van Loon to Detroit by train, found bands and waving flags on the platform and feared his ruse had not worked. However, the duo quickly (and ruefully) discovered that the commotion was to welcome cartoonist George McManus—not a children's book author!

At the ceremony that afternoon, Melcher spoke first, presenting the medal to Clara Hunt, the section chair, who in turn bestowed it on van Loon. The only record of his acceptance speech states: "Dr. van Loon responded in merry vein" (Miller and Field 1955). On leaving the stage, the three were surrounded by a flurry of reporters and photographers. Van Loon's popularity with adult readers and his name recognition provided a conspicuous debut for the new award.

Before the conference ended the Children's Librarians' Section drew up a resolution expressing gratitude to Melcher for "his generosity which prompted the gift and saw it executed in so beautiful and worthy a fashion" (Smith 1957). The following November, Melcher drafted a full statement of the medal's origins and intent, outlining all aspects of the award, including details about the recipient, the method, the purpose, and the name. It was presented to the ALA Executive Board, which voted to accept Melcher's document on December 27, 1922—making the John Newbery Award official.

As always with a fledgling award, rules and regulations were changed, delineated, and refined in the ensuing years. In 1924, the section concluded that a special award committee, instead of a popular vote, should decide the winner. It would consist of the section's executive committee, the book evaluation committee, and three members at large. That made Charles Finger (*Tales from Silver Lands,* Doubleday, 1924) the first person to be chosen by a committee designed for the purpose of choosing a Newbery Medal winner.

In 1929, the Newbery Committee was enlarged to fifteen: four current officers, the ex-chair, and the chairs of the standing committees. Although nominations were still encouraged, it had become obvious when only 150 suggestions were received the year before that the process worked best as a committee endeavor.

Back in June of 1921 when Melcher first presented his award idea, the librarians' enthusiasm reverberated across the hotel's veranda. According to Clara Hunt, if the award had been decided at that moment, Hugh Lofting's *The Story of Doctor Dolittle* (Frederick A. Stokes, 1920), published that year, would have been named the winner

(Smith 1957). In 1923, Lofting *did* win a Newbery—the second medal to be given—for *The Voyages of Doctor Dolittle* (Frederick A. Stokes, 1922).

The Dolittle tales feature an eccentric country doctor with a bent for natural history and a unique ability to talk to animals. In *Voyages,* Doctor Dolittle sails to Spider Monkey Island, where he unites two tribes, becomes king, and sails home inside a 70,000-year-old glass sea snail. Readers praised Lofting's storytelling talent as well as his natural ability to speak—through Dr. Dolittle—to readers young and old.

Born in England, Lofting had immigrated to the United States, but at the outbreak of World War I, he left his family with relatives in England and joined the Irish Guards. While serving at the front, he became disheartened over the sorry treatment of the horses and mules under fire. In illustrated letters to his children, Lofting invented a doctor who would do for the animals what was not and could not be done in real life. His son became so entranced with the stories that he began calling himself Dr. Dolittle. Injured and sent home, Lofting met author Cecil Roberts (whose novels about New England are still held in high regard) on a transatlantic trip back to America. Upon hearing the stories (and meeting "Dr. Dolittle"), Roberts recommended Lofting to his publisher, Frederick A. Stokes, who published Lofting's books to great acclaim. The extremely popular series grew to fourteen titles, but today children are more familiar with the Dr. Dolittle of the 1967 film (often shown on television) starring Rex Harrison and the 1998 and 2001 films featuring Eddie Murphy.

The third Newbery winner (1924) was Charles Boardman Hawes. *The Dark Frigate* (Little, Brown, 1923), a tale of rugged life on the high seas in which young Philip is forced into joining a pirate crew, was Hawes's third book. Born in New York in 1889, Hawes was the first American-born Newbery winner. He worked as a writer, educator, and editor and had drawn attention as a promising young author: his first writing effort, *The Mutineers* (Little, Brown, 1920), received good reviews, and his second book, *The Great Quest,* was a 1922 Honor Book. Hawes's career, unfortunately, was cut short when he died suddenly at age 34, never knowing *The Dark Frigate* had claimed a Newbery Medal. At the ALA conference in Saratoga Springs, the third John Newbery Award ceremony was a bittersweet affair. Hawes's wife gave a short appreciative speech, then accepted her husband's award to a standing ovation.

Illustrations for Hawes's *The Dark Frigate* have an interesting background. Published with a frontispiece and eight black-and-white illustrations, the book contains only the word "Illustrated" on the title page. Anton Otto Fischer has been credited with the work in many major sources. Close examination of a first edition, however, reveals the name A. L. Ripley on the frontispiece and the initials A.L.R. on all eight line drawings. Ripley did, in fact, illustrate children's books, including Arthur Walden's *Leading a Dog's Life* (Houghton, 1931) and Horacio Quiroga's *South American Jungle Tales* (Dodd, Mead, 1943), leading one to assume that, in a work-for-hire situation, he did the artwork but was not credited.

When Little, Brown reissued *The Dark Frigate* in 1934, they substituted a full-color illustration by Anton Otto Fischer on the frontispiece, dropped the black-and-white line drawings, and gave Fischer credit on the title page. In 1996, the book was again released, this time without a frontispiece but with decorations by Warren Chappell topping each chapter.

The 1925 winner—Charles J. Finger for *Tales from Silver Lands*—is filled with stories of exotic adventures from the author's own life. In his autobiography, *Seven Horizons* (Doubleday, 1930), Finger recounts the ten amazing years he spent in Tierra del Fuego and Patagonia. Back home in Arkansas, he retold the stories he had heard around the South American campfires to his wife and five children. Later, at his typewriter, those tales of jungle animals, sea creatures, fairy sprites, and earth people that seemed to flow directly from the mouths of the native storytellers became *Tales from Silver Lands*. His wife described him as a "weaver of fairy tales" in a tribute following his death.

A book similar in nature, *Shen of the Sea: A Book for Children* (Dutton, 1925), by Arthur Bowie Chrisman, captured the Newbery the following year. Folk and wonder tales are again at the heart of the book, but here they take on a Chinese flavor. Although he never traveled to China, Chrisman spent many years in California, exploring the state on foot. During his travels he befriended a Chinese shopkeeper who could, Chrisman said, sometimes be persuaded to "put on his talking cap." Through their long conversations, Chrisman became intrigued by Chinese history and literature, and strains of this interest crept into his books and stories.

In *Newbery Medal Books 1922–1955,* Chrisman, a prolific writer, authored the highly laudatory "Book Note" about Will James's *Smoky, the Cowhorse* (Scribner, 1926), the 1927 Newbery Medal winner. Chrisman describes James's surprising relationship with his editor—the renowned Maxwell Perkins, who nursed such luminaries as Thomas Wolfe, Ernest Hemingway, and Marjorie Kinnan Rawlings into print. The elitist Perkins, it seems, treasured the ten-gallon hat given to him by James and found the authentic American vernacular of James's writing highly likable.

Orphaned at age four, James was taken in by a Canadian trapper who "taught him to read and write a little." A cowboy with a quick wit, James was amazed to find *Smoky* winning the Newbery, saying it had been published as a book for adults. "I don't know about that Medal, but it's fine with me." Some librarians criticized the book as too full of "cowboy lingo," saying that boys and girls would never read it. Others (among them undoubtedly the Newbery committee) found it "a bit of poetry in disguise," full of humor, color, and excitement. The story did in fact prove highly popular and continual reprints necessitated new plates in 1955.

Dhan Gopal Mukerji's *Gay-Neck, the Story of a Pigeon* (Dutton, 1927), the 1928 Newbery Medal winner, tells of the training and care of a carrier pigeon. Writing out of his own experiences, Mukerji tells how Gay-Neck's master sent his prized bird to serve in France during World War I to carry messages of courage and hope, eventually welcoming him home as a hero. Incidents from Mukerji's own boyhood are woven into a theme that proclaims man and winged animals as brothers. Mukerji, the son of Brahmin parents, immigrated to America at age 19, attended Stanford University, married an American, and spent the rest of his life in the United States writing for both adults and children, until his death by suicide in 1936.

The final 1920s Newbery winner was Eric Philbrook Kelly's *The Trumpeter of Krakow: A Tale of the Fifteenth Century* (Macmillan, 1928). While in Europe following World War I, Kelly visited Poland and developed a strong rapport with the Polish people. He returned later to teach and study at the University of Krakow and became motivated to write a story about the city. Its absolute charm and history, he said, led him to set the novel in medieval times. The writing of the book, Kelly said, "launched me into the destiny of a new nation" (Miller and Field 1955). After World War II, asked by the U.S. Department of State to help resettle Polish refugees in Mexico, he founded a refuge for homeless Poles, half of them children, in an abandoned hacienda in León, Mexico. He eventually returned to Dartmouth, where he went on to write other books—but, he said, his intoxication with Krakow never left him.

While the 1920s Newbery Medals were completely male dominated, nine women did capture Honor Book designations during those first years. Most of those titles are little known and long out of print, with the notable exception of Wanda Gág's *Millions of Cats* (Coward, 1928), which received a Newbery Honor in 1929 and has been continuously in print since its publication.

Studying these early Newbery Medal and Honor Book authors—who they were, what they wrote, what influenced their writing—is absorbing and revealing. These twenty-one men and women set the stage for the decades to follow, where winners selected from ever-growing choices of books stand proudly, having been proclaimed "distinguished" for their literary merit.

SOURCES

Mahony, Bertha E. 1947. *Illustrators of Children's Books: 1744–1945*. The Horn Book.

Miller, Bertha Mahony, and Elinor Whitney Field. 1955. *Newbery Medal Books: 1922–1955*. The Horn Book.

Smith, Irene. 1957. *A History of the Newbery and Caldecott Medals*. Viking.

Unitarian Universalist Historical Society. http://www.uua.org/uuhs/duub/articles/hendrikwillemvanloon.html.

The Newbery Awards

2007–1922

2007 NEWBERY AWARD

THE HIGHER POWER OF LUCKY
Susan Patron
Illustrated by Matt Phelan
Atheneum/Richard Jackson Books

SUSAN PATRON

Patron takes readers to the California desert community of Hard Pan (population 43), where ten-year-old Lucky Trimble eavesdrops on twelve-step program meetings from her hiding place behind Hard Pan's Found Object Wind Chime Museum & Visitor Center. Eccentric characters and quirky details spice up Lucky's life just as fresh parsley embellishes her guardian Brigitte's French cuisine.

"*Lucky* is a perfectly nuanced blend of adventure, survival (emotional and physical), and hilarious character study . . . as well as a blueprint for a self-examined life," said Newbery Medal Committee Chair Jeri Kladder. "Through Lucky's experiences, we are reminded that children support one another just as needy adults do."

2007 HONOR BOOKS

Penny from Heaven   Jennifer L. Holm
Random House

Eleven-year-old Penny looks forward to spending the summer rooting for the Brooklyn Dodgers and scheming with her cousin Frankie. Instead she navigates the space between her two families and uncovers the reason for their estrangement in this funny and touching tale of intergenerational love set in 1953.

Hattie Big Sky   Kirby Larson
Delacorte

Sixteen-year-old orphan Hattie Brooks is looking for a place to belong—a home. In 1918 she leaves Iowa for the Montana prairie. In this engaging first-person narrative, Hattie strives to forge a new life. Vivid imagery and careful attention to historical detail distinguish this memorable novel that portrays her struggle to "prove her claim."

Rules   Cynthia Lord
Scholastic

"A boy can take off his shirt to swim, but not his shorts." Twelve-year-old Catherine creates rules for her younger, autistic brother David in an attempt to normalize his life and her own; but what is normal? In her debut novel, Lord's heroine learns to use words to forge connections with her brother, her workaholic father, and a paraplegic friend. With humor and insight, Lord demonstrates the transforming power of language.

2006 AWARD

Criss Cross   Lynne Rae Perkins   Greenwillow

Criss Cross follows the lives of four fourteen-year-olds in a small town. Each at their own crossroads, this ensemble cast explores new thoughts and feelings in their quest to find the meaning of life and love. In thirty-eight brief chapters, this poetic, postmodern novel experiments with a variety of styles: haiku, song lyrics, question-and-answer dialogue, and split-screen scenarios.

HONORS

Whittington   Alan Armstrong
Illustrated by S. D. Schindler   Random House

> Armstrong creates a glorious barnyard fantasy that seamlessly weaves together three tales: Whittington the cat's arrival on Bernie's farm, his retelling of the traditional legend of his fourteenth-century namesake, and one boy's struggle to learn to read. The tales unite the disparate citizens of the barn community in a celebration of oral and written language, the support of friends, the healing power of humor, and the triumph of life.

Hitler Youth: Growing Up in Hitler's Shadow
Susan Campbell Bartoletti   Scholastic

> How could the Holocaust have happened? Bartoletti delivers a chilling answer by exploring Hitler's rise to power through the firsthand experiences of young followers whose adolescent zeal he so successfully exploited and the more extraordinary few who risked certain death in resisting. The meticulously researched volume traces the Hitler Youth movement from the early 1930s through the defeat of the Third Reich.

Princess Academy   Shannon Hale   Bloomsbury Children's Books

> Miri and the other young women of her rocky highland village are forced to leave their close-knit community when the prince must choose a bride. Miri soon becomes the strong, resilient, and courageous leader of the academy. The book is a fresh approach to the traditional princess story with unexpected plot twists and great emotional resonance.

Show Way   Jacqueline Woodson   Illustrated by Hudson Talbott   Putnam

> Jacqueline Woodson's magnificent poem "Show Way" tells the story of slavery, emancipation, and triumph for each generation of her maternal ancestors. She pays tribute to the creative women who guided their "tall and straight-boned" daughters to courage, self-sufficiency, and freedom. Whether with quilts or stories, poems or songs, these women discovered and shared the strength to carry on.

2005 AWARD

Kira-Kira   Cynthia Kadohata   Atheneum

Two sisters lie on their backs, watching the stars and repeating the Japanese word for "glittering"—"kira-kira." Like this quiet opening scene, Kadohata's tenderly nuanced novel glitters with plain and poignant words that describe the strong love within a Japanese American family from the point of view of younger sister Katie. Personal challenges and family tragedy are set against the oppressive social climate of the South during the 1950s and early 1960s.

HONORS

Al Capone Does My Shirts   Gennifer Choldenko   Putnam

> With Alcatraz as the evocative backdrop for this highly original novel set in 1935, twelve-year-old Moose Flanagan tells about the travails of "the Rock," where his father has taken a job. Hilarious antics are deftly interwoven with themes of isolation and imprisonment, compassion and connection.

The Voice That Challenged a Nation: Marian Anderson and the Struggle for Equal Rights   Russell Freedman   Clarion

> *The Voice That Challenged a Nation* meticulously explores resonant themes with the masterful structure of a musical composition. Eloquent, economic prose sheds a personal light on one woman's sometimes reluctant role as a symbol in the struggle against racism and her calling to share an illustrious gift.

Lizzie Bright and the Buckminster Boy   Gary D. Schmidt   Clarion

> Set in Maine in 1912 and propelled by a tragic historical event, Schmidt's powerfully haunting novel probes a forbidden friendship between a preacher's son and a dark-skinned girl from a nearby island. Steeped in imagery and laced with surprising humor, *Lizzie Bright and the Buckminster Boy* explores powerlessness, possibility, and the profound impact individuals can make.

2004 AWARD

The Tale of Despereaux: Being the Story of a Mouse, a Princess, Some Soup, and a Spool of Thread   Kate DiCamillo
Illustrated by Timothy Basil Ering   Candlewick

The Tale of Despereaux draws the reader into an enchanting account of a smaller-than-usual mouse in love with music, stories, and a princess named Pea. With character and plot far more complex than the traditional fairy tale, separate stories introduce

Despereaux, condemned for talking to the princess; the evil rat, Roscuro, who loves light and soup; and Miggery Sow, a farm girl with royal aspirations. Their fates are threaded together as Despereaux undertakes a hero's quest that culminates in mice, rats, and humans living almost happily ever after.

HONORS

Olive's Ocean   Kevin Henkes   Greenwillow

> Twelve-year-old Martha receives a page from the journal of a classmate, Olive, who has died in an accident. Olive's entry about a desire to be Martha's friend, to see the ocean, and to become a writer propels Martha into a journey from childhood to the brink of adolescence.

An American Plague: The True and Terrifying Story
of the Yellow Fever Epidemic of 1793   Jim Murphy   Clarion

> *An American Plague: The True and Terrifying Story of the Yellow Fever Epidemic of 1793* dramatically recounts the story of the yellow fever epidemic that nearly decimated the population of Philadelphia at the end of the eighteenth century. Integrating newspapers, diaries, personal testimonies, and period illustrations, the narrative delivers a social and medical history of the times and raises chilling questions about the disease today.

2003 AWARD

Crispin: The Cross of Lead   Avi   Hyperion

Crispin: The Cross of Lead is an action-filled page-turner set in fourteenth-century England. "Asta's son" is the only name the thirteen-year-old title character has ever known when he is suddenly orphaned and stripped of home and possessions. Accused of murder and wanted dead or alive, Crispin flees his village and falls in with a juggler, Bear, who becomes his protector and teacher. Relentlessly pursued by Crispin's enemies, the pair flees to solve the mystery of his identity and fight the injustices of feudalism.

HONORS

The House of the Scorpion   Nancy Farmer   Richard Jackson/Atheneum

> Farmer tackles the provocative topics of cloning, the value of life, illegal immigration, and the drug trade in a coming-of-age novel set in a desolate, futuristic desert.

Pictures of Hollis Woods   Patricia Reilly Giff   Random House

> Twelve-year-old Hollis Woods unfolds her story of foster care and a search for family in images from her sketchbook, which reveal both her memories and her

artistic soul. Strong visual imagery, multi-layered structure, and memorable characters create an emotionally satisfying story.

Hoot   Carl Hiaasen   Knopf

Hiaasen's wildly funny satire features the new kid, Roy, joining forces with tough Beatrice and the elusive Mullet Fingers to defeat a bully, thwart an avaricious corporation, and save a colony of burrowing owls. Hiaasen's work is both a rollicking adventure and a serious examination of values that threaten our environment.

A Corner of the Universe   Ann M. Martin   Scholastic

With the surprising arrival of a mentally disabled uncle, twelve-year-old Hattie Owen's world is turned upside down. Ann Martin used her own childhood memories to create a 1960s small-town setting, perfectly suited to this poignant story.

Surviving the Applewhites   Stephanie S. Tolan   HarperCollins

Tolan features pierced and spike-haired Jake, who has been expelled from every possible public school before his unwilling arrival at Wit's End, N.C., and the homeschool run by the chaotic and outrageous Applewhite family. The eccentric characters and fast pace culminate in a hilarious musical production that forces Jake to grow.

2002 AWARD

A Single Shard   Linda Sue Park   Clarion

Park takes readers to twelfth-century Korea to tell a timeless story of dedication to one's dreams and art in *A Single Shard*. Tree-ear, an orphan, becomes fascinated with a nearby community of potters. Drawn by their exquisite craftsmanship, the adolescent boy begins to assist the master potter Min. Tree-ear's determination and bravery in pursuing his dream of becoming a potter take readers on a literary journey that demonstrates how courage, honor, and perseverance can overcome great odds and bring great happiness.

HONORS

Everything on a Waffle   Polly Horvath   Farrar Straus Giroux

When eleven-year-old Primrose Squarp's parents disappear at sea, her faith in their return defies all adult logic. Set in British Columbia, *Everything on a Waffle* combines quirky characters, recipes, and amazing twists of plot in a striking combination of the barely credible and profoundly true.

Carver: A Life in Poems   Marilyn Nelson   Front Street

Nelson challenges readers with a truly new biography of George Washington Carver. Told from multiple perspectives, this collection of fifty-nine poems reveals little-known facets of the remarkable scientist, who it too often dismissed as "the peanut man." With simple sophistication and beauty, Nelson transcends Carver's brilliance and scientific achievements to present the essence of this profoundly humble man.

2001 AWARD

A Year Down Yonder   Richard Peck   Dial

A linked series of vignettes set in rural Illinois during the Depression. *A Year Down Yonder* tells the story of fifteen-year-old Mary Alice who leaves Chicago to spend a year with Grandma Dowdel. Her initial apprehension about life in a small town with a scheming old woman gradually gives way to admiration and love as she recognizes the warm heart behind Grandma's shenanigans.

HONORS

Hope Was Here   Joan Bauer   Putnam

Hope Was Here relates how sixteen-year-old Hope and her aunt move to a small town in Wisconsin to join the "short order dance" of life at the Welcome Stairways Diner. In the course of just a few months, Hope encounters issues as diverse as her customers: corruption in politics, a new love, serious illness, and the meaning of family.

The Wanderer   Sharon Creech   JoannaCotler/HarperCollins

Sailing across the Atlantic with her uncles and cousins becomes a journey of discovery for thirteen-year-old Sophie. The carefully designed plot gradually reveals the truth of Sophie's past, even as readers begin to wonder about this rag-tag crew. Through journal entries, multiple viewpoints are weaved into a story that speaks to the power of survival and the delicacy of grief.

Because of Winn-Dixie   Kate DiCamillo   Candlewick

When a stray dog appears almost magically in the midst of the produce section of the Winn-Dixie grocery store, he leads ten-year-old India Opal Buloni from one new friend to the next in a small Florida town. The stories she hears from each one help her to piece together a new definition of family.

Joey Pigza Loses Control   Jack Gantos   Farrar Straus Giroux

Spending the summer with his estranged father, Joey longs for the two of them to be winners together, but their lives gradually spiral out of control. As the old "wired" Joey returns, readers will long to see him regain his balance in an out-of-kilter world. Like many family stories, this is a tale whose pain is generously laced with humor.

2000 AWARD

Bud, Not Buddy   Christopher Paul Curtis   Delacorte

Ten-year-old Bud Caldwell runs away from a foster home and begins an unforgettable journey in search of his father. His only clues are old flyers left by his now-deceased mother that point to a legendary jazz bandleader. Bud's fast-paced first-person account moves with the rhythms of jazz and celebrates life, family, and a child's indomitable spirit.

HONORS

Getting Near to Baby   Audrey Couloumbis   Putnam

Twelve-year-old Willa Jo and Little Sister, whose voice is "lost in sadness," live with bossy Aunt Patty following the death of their baby sister. Willa Jo finds haven on the roof and from sunrise to sunset recalls recent events and helps her family come to terms with its tragedy.

Our Only May Amelia   Jennifer L. Holm   HarperCollins

Growing up as the only girl in a large Finnish-American farming family along Washington's Nasel River in 1899, 12-year-old May Amelia prefers tricks and adventures to being a "proper young lady." Unjustly blamed for tragedy, May must leave home before returning to claim her rightful place.

26 Fairmount Avenue   Tomie dePaola   Illustrated by the author   Putnam

DePaola looks back to 1938 when his family, overcoming fire and flood, builds a new house. That year Tomie "quits" kindergarten, shares "chocolates" with Nana upstairs, critiques a movie, practices mural art, and finally moves to 26 Fairmount Avenue.

1999 AWARD

Holes   Louis Sachar   Frances Foster/Farrar Straus Giroux

Stanley Yelnats, the heir to his family's curse of bad luck, is convicted of a crime he didn't commit. He serves his sentence at Camp Green Lake, a dry, flat wasteland where the warden assigns each inmate the task of digging one hole every day. Hole by hole, Stanley and his friend Zero dig their destiny.

HONOR

A Long Way from Chicago: A Novel in Stories   Richard Peck   Dial

>An old man looks back on rollicking summers spent with his larger-than-life grandmother during the Great Depression in this colorful novel made up of seven masterfully interwoven tales.

1998 AWARD

Out of the Dust   Karen Hesse   Scholastic

Fourteen-year-old Billie Jo relates how her mother dies after an accident with burning kerosene. Blaming both herself and her father, she is unable to express herself through her piano playing because of the burns that scar her hands. She leaves but quickly returns to her home "of dust" and she realizes how much a part of her it is.

HONORS

Ella Enchanted   Gail Carson Levine   HarperCollins

>Spunky, stubborn, and very clever, this new Cinderella spends a lifetime trying to outwit the curse of a fairy's unwelcome gift of obedience. In a kingdom populated with ogres, giants, princes, and fairies, Ella begins a fruitless quest to have the curse lifted, only to discover that she has that power within herself.

Lily's Crossing   Patricia Reilly Giff   Delacorte

>During her 1944 summer vacation in the Rockaways, ten-year-old Lily's best friend moves away and her beloved father Poppy goes off to war. Then Lily meets Albert, a young Hungarian refugee with whom she builds a poignant friendship based on shared loneliness, secrets, and lies.

Wringer   Jerry Spinelli   Joanna Cotler/HarperCollins

>Palmer LaRue dreads his approaching birthday because he does not want to be a wringer, one of the ten-year-old boys who breaks the necks of pigeons wounded at the town's pigeon shoot fund-raiser. When his three bullying friends suspect he is sheltering a stray pigeon, Palmer decides to take a personal stand against this annual rite of passage.

1997 AWARD

The View from Saturday   E. L. Konigsburg   Jean Karl/Atheneum

Mrs. Olinski selects four of her sixth-grade students to be the Academic Bowl team. No one understands her choice of these particular students, including Mrs. Olinski, who continues to question herself. The students surprise everyone with their unique contributions to the challenges of competition.

HONORS

A Girl Named Disaster   Nancy Farmer   Orchard

When Nhamo (Disaster) flees her village to search for her father in Zimbabwe, she is lost on Lake Cabora Bassa in Mozambique. Alone, she survives harsh weather, wild animals, and near starvation before building a new life in the world of her father's people.

Moorchild   Eloise McGraw   Margaret K. McElderry Books

Moorchild Moql becomes the changeling Saaski, half-human, half-Folk, and an outcast in both worlds. The reader is drawn into the lives of the moorfolk who fear Saaski and those who try to understand her and support her.

The Thief   Megan Whalen Turner   Greenwillow

Freed from the royal dungeons and commanded to steal an ancient talisman from supernatural guardians, young Gen pulls off an astonishing scam and in the process rescues his own country from a threatened invasion.

Belle Prater's Boy   Ruth White   Farrar Straus Giroux

Gypsy's cousin Woodrow comes to live next door, bringing with him a mystery and the key to a secret that Gypsy keeps from herself. Grandparents and Gypsy's supportive mother and stepfather create a loving environment in which the children can come to grips with their losses.

1996 AWARD

The Midwife's Apprentice   Karen Cushman   Clarion

The central character, Brat, is a homeless waif who first appears sleeping in a dung heap "unwashed, unnourished, unloved, and unlovely. . . ." From a person with no hopes, no dreams, and no expectations she becomes the midwife's apprentice—a person with a name and a place in the world. An excellent portrayal of medieval England.

HONORS

What Jamie Saw   Carolyn Coman   Front Street

> *What Jamie Saw* is a gripping interior novel that portrays a desperate mother and her quietly heroic son as they move from an impossibly bleak situation toward a promise of hope. Coman captures Jamie's fear, his uncertainty, and his confusion as well as his growing confidence and ability to stand up for himself.

The Watsons Go to Birmingham—1963   Christopher Paul Curtis   Delacorte

> From its hilarious opening chapters to its shattering conclusion, *The Watsons Go to Birmingham* is a compelling novel that brings to life an African-American family. It draws together everyday events in such a way as to send the Watsons on a journey to Birmingham that will change them forever. The depiction of devastating events in Birmingham integrates the dichotomy of familial love and stability with the racial strife of the 1960s.

Yolonda's Genius   Carol Fenner   Margaret K. McElderry Books

> Fenner portrays memorable characters and a vivid, authentic place in this engaging story of a bright, feisty fifth grader. Yolonda is determined to bring to light her younger brother's extraordinary talent of transforming the world around him into the music he makes.

The Great Fire   Jim Murphy   Scholastic

> The riveting narrative of the 1871 Chicago fire thrusts the reader into the center of the raging conflagration. Murphy weaves eyewitness accounts of the disaster with factual and social commentary, period photographs, etchings, and maps into memorable nonfiction writing.

1995 AWARD

Walk Two Moons   Sharon Creech   HarperCollins

Thirteen-year-old Salamanca Tree Hiddle sets out on a cross-country journey with her grandparents to see her mother, who has not returned from a visit to Idaho. Sal entertains her grandparents by telling them about her new friend Phoebe, and in so doing begins to understand herself and her own mother. The book, packed with humor and affection, is an odyssey of unexpected twists and surprising conclusions.

HONORS

Catherine, Called Birdy   Karen Cushman   Clarion

> In the course of her fourteenth year, Catherine keeps a journal of her perceptive observations and longings for adventure and independence. Her lively, humorous

descriptions of life on a thirteenth century English manor, midst unwanted suitors and ever-present fleas, reach through to time to speak to modern readers.

The Ear, the Eye, and the Arm   Nancy Farmer   Orchard

A kidnapping of the General's three children in twenty-second-century Zimbabwe sets off a dramatic chase. In a series of extraordinary adventures, the children play a crucial role in a thrilling battle against the forces of evil. This futuristic detective story is interwoven with African's history, present-day concerns, and a variety of colorful characters.

1994 AWARD

The Giver   Lois Lowry   Houghton

Twelve-year-old Jonas performs well in the impressively ordered society that the Elders have developed. But when he is selected to be the new "Receiver," Jonas begins to unravel the truth that underlies his world.

HONORS

Crazy Lady!   Jane Leslie Conly   Laura Geringer/HarperCollins

Twelve-year-old Vernon's initially reluctant, off-beat friendship with an alcoholic and her developmentally disabled son has repercussions throughout the neighborhood, changing the lives of all involved. The reader becomes aware that Vernon's growing self-esteem and maturity come about through his commitment to helping his friends.

Eleanor Roosevelt: A Life of Discovery   Russell Freedman   Clarion

Through compelling text and contemporary photographs, Eleanor Roosevelt is shown moving from a sheltered, unhappy childhood to the world's stage. This fascinating biography of a remarkable and complex woman is meticulously researched.

Dragon's Gate   Laurence Yep   HarperCollins

Dragon's Gate is a carefully researched, well-written account of the lives of the Chinese who built the transcontinental railroad in the Sierra Mountains. This glimpse into the complex working community of California at the time of the Civil War is also a sensitive portrayal of the relationship between a father and son.

1993 AWARD

Missing May   Cynthia Rylant   Orchard

Twelve-year-old Summer lives with her Aunt May and Uncle Ob in the mountains of West Virginia. When May dies, Summer, Uncle Ob, and Summer's friend, Cletus, try to get her back—or at least to get word of her—and to alleviate the pain. This trio of lovingly described characters journeys from intense grief to the understanding that love is never truly lost.

HONORS

What Hearts   Bruce Brooks   Laura Geringer/HarperCollins

Seven-year-old Asa, by far the best in his class, comes home from the last day of school with a knapsack full of prizes to find that his whole world has changed. Asa tries to make sense of a world in which he is challenged and put down by a domineering stepfather and only partially sustained by his loving but disturbed mother. Four stories show Asa at seven, nine, eleven, and twelve, struggling to find the secret of connection with others.

The Dark-thirty: Southern Tales of the Supernatural
Patricia C. McKissack   Knopf

The dark-thirty is that special half hour of twilight, just before dark, when everyone hurries home because the spirits and monsters come out. This collection of spine-tingling tales ranges from the time of slavery to the civil rights movement. Strong characterization, classic themes, and suspenseful plots are strongly crafted in the oral tradition of African-American folklore.

Somewhere in the Darkness   Walter Dean Myers   Scholastic

Jimmy Little had always wanted a father. However, when Crab, his father, who is virtually a stranger, appears in a dark hallway straight from a prison hospital, it is not at all what he had hoped for. On the tense, frightening trip with Crab to Chicago and then to Alabama, Jimmy finds he must learn self-knowledge as well as compassion to deal with a difficult and dangerous situation.

1992 AWARD

Shiloh   Phyllis Reynolds Naylor   Atheneum

Marty Preston, an eleven-year-old West Virginian boy, befriends a stray dog and while protecting the dog from abuse wrestles with universal questions of honesty, commitment, and ethical decision making. Marty discovers that discerning right from wrong is not as straightforward as he had imagined.

HONORS

Nothing But the Truth: A Documentary Novel   Avi   Orchard

Avi's documentary approach chronicles the results of a teacher's objection to a ninth grader's humming along with "The Star Spangled Banner." School rules stipulate that students are to stand at "respectful, silent attention." Miscommunication, misperceptions, and personal viewpoints of right, wrong, and protected freedoms propel the characters rapidly into a crisis situation that forces the reader to explore issues of perception, reality, bias, and expediency.

The Wright Brothers: How They Invented the Airplane
Russell Freedman   Illustrated with original photographs
by Wilbur and Orville Wright   Holiday House

In a spirited blend of science, history, and biography, Freedman presents a fascinating portrait of a new age. Using Wilber and Orville Wright's own photographs as well as excerpts from their notes and journals, he creates a uniquely personal and engaging view of their accomplishments.

1991 AWARD

Maniac Magee   Jerry Spinelli   Little, Brown

Jeffrey Lionel Magee is a legendary character who runs the rails faster than other kids run the ground. Jeffrey bunts "the world's first frogball for a four-bagger" and performs other amazing feats.

HONOR

The True Confessions of Charlotte Doyle   Avi   Orchard

Avi weaves a finely crafted tale of high seas adventure and gripping suspense, made rich by thirteen-year-old Charlotte's deepening understanding of honor and herself.

1990 AWARD

Number the Stars   Lois Lowry   Houghton

When ten-year-old Annemarie Johansen's family decides to pretend that her friend Ellen Rosen is her sister, they become involved in the effort to save the Danish Jews from the Nazis. As the author deftly portrays deep friendship, a strong family, and heroism in wartime, the story builds to a tense climax.

HONORS

Afternoon of the Elves   Janet Taylor Lisle   Orchard

Fascinated by Sarah-Kate's backyard elf village, Hillary is unprepared for the secret side of the older girl's life. Strong, tough, an outcast at school, Sarah-Kate has been doing whatever she must to care for herself and her mentally ill mother. When her plight is discovered by adults, disturbing but necessary changes occur.

The Winter Room   Gary Paulsen   Orchard

From the first page to the last, this story of farm life in northern Minnesota is so engrossing that the place and the people seem real. Eldon, the eleven-year-old narrator, takes the reader through the seasons and into the winter room, where stories are "not for believing so much, as to be believed in."

Shabanu, Daughter of the Wind   Suzanne Fisher Staples   Knopf

Spirited and courageous Shabanu, younger daughter of present-day Pakistani camel herders, loves her family's life and her role in caring for their camels. Both Shabanu and her older sister are betrothed to brothers, but as her sister's wedding nears, a calamity occurs that changes forever the life of independent Shabanu.

1989 AWARD

Joyful Noise: Poems for Two Voices   Paul Fleischman
Illustrated by Eric Beddows   Charlotte Zolotow/Harper & Row

Fourteen poems, using two voices, sometimes alternating, sometimes together, offer listeners a look at what insects just might think of themselves and their world. The book lice, grasshoppers, house crickets, and their poetic companions are illustrated in soft yet often comical black-and-white pencil drawings.

HONORS

In the Beginning: Creation Stories from Around the World
Virginia Hamilton   Illustrated by Barry Moser   Harcourt Brace Jovanovich

Stories from African, Chinese, Native American, and Guinean peoples are represented among the twenty-five creation myths found in this collection. Faithfully retold, the stories are followed by notes about their sources. Dramatic watercolor paintings accent each tale.

Scorpions   Walter Dean Myers   Harper & Row

Hoping to find a way to raise money for an appeal for his imprisoned older brother, twelve-year-old Jamal agrees to try to become the leader of his brother's Harlem gang, the Scorpions. Involvement with the gang (and the gun he is given) leads to tragedy for Jamal and his friend Tito.

1988 AWARD

Lincoln: A Photobiography   Russell Freedman   Clarion

An ambitious man, Lincoln struggled hard to get an education, to build his law practice, and to become politically successful. The man, his wit, and his wisdom are vividly and honestly portrayed in this straightforward biography and its ninety photographs.

HONORS

After the Rain   Norma Fox Mazer   Morrow

Fifteen-year-old Rachel tries to balance her concern for her own life with her grandfather's need for her help. Never close to the old man, she slowly comes to love him. As she struggles to help him maintain his independence, he weakens and nears death.

Hatchet   Gary Paulsen   Bradbury

When the pilot dies of a heart attack, Brian crash-lands the small plane in the Canadian wilderness. Left with only a hatchet and the clothes he is wearing, Brian begins a gripping fifty-four-day ordeal that challenges his physical and psychological skills to their limits.

1987 AWARD

The Whipping Boy   Sid Fleischman   Illustrated by Peter Sís   Greenwillow

Whenever Prince Brat does anything bad, Jemmy, his whipping boy, is punished. The spoiled prince decides to run away from the palace, forcing Jemmy to go with him. Far from the safety of the court, the prince quickly learns how little he knows about the outside world and how important Jemmy is to his survival.

HONORS

On My Honor   Marion Dane Bauer   Clarion

Before leaving on a bike ride with his impetuous friend Tony, Joel gives his father his word of honor that he will not swim in a river known to be dangerous. Tony convinces Joel that the river is safe; the two swim; and Tony drowns. Joel is left alone to face his guilt, both sets of parents, and his own grief.

Volcano: The Eruption and Healing of Mount St. Helens
Patricia Lauber   Bradbury

The eruption of Mount St. Helens and the subsequent regrowth of plants are vividly portrayed in color photographs and a dynamic text. The volcanic eruption is seen not as just a disaster, but as a builder of life on this planet.

A Fine White Dust   Cynthia Rylant   Bradbury

Although neither his parents nor his best friend are particularly religious, Peter feels a need for something deeper than just churchgoing. When an itinerant preacher comes to town, Peter is mesmerized by the man and "saved." Invited to go away with the preacher, Peter reluctantly agrees, only to be left behind and forgotten.

1986 AWARD

Sarah, Plain and Tall   Patricia MacLachlan   Harper & Row

Life on the prairie with two children and no wife is lonely and difficult, so Caleb and Anna's father advertises for a wife. Sarah answers his ad and soon agrees to come all the way from Maine for a visit. Captivated by her, Anna and Caleb worry that Sarah misses the sea too much to stay with them.

HONORS

Commodore Perry in the Land of the Shogun   Rhoda Blumberg   Lothrop

Commodore Perry's fascinating mission to Japan in 1853 is told at a lively pace, with special attention given to the negotiating skill that led to his success; to his sensitivity to cultural differences; and to his just plain curiosity. The accompanying pictures include many sketched by the Japanese and the Americans who were with Matthew Perry.

Dogsong   Gary Paulsen   Bradbury

Unhappy with the snowmobile-and-television society that seems to have taken over his Eskimo village, Russell turns to Oogruk, the old man of the village, for help in finding a path back to the old ways. With Oogruk's advice and encouragement, Russell begins an arduous dogsled journey northward to find his own "song."

1985 AWARD

The Hero and the Crown   Robin McKinley   Greenwillow

The daughter of the king of Damar and his second wife (a witch woman from the north), Aerin does not fit in at court. Unable to succeed her father to the throne, she must instead find her own destiny. Wielding her blue sword, she not only defeats dragons but finally becomes the hero of the kingdom.

HONORS

The Moves Make the Man   Bruce Brooks   Harper & Row

The first black to go to the formerly all-white junior high school, Jerome is a passionate basketball player. When he meets Bix Rivers, an unstable outsider who is a gifted athlete, Jerome decides to teach him basketball. As they play the game, Bix's mental illness becomes more apparent, and Jerome is less able to help him.

One-Eyed Cat   Paula Fox   Bradbury

After his minister father takes his new air rifle away from him and puts it in the attic, Ned sneaks upstairs, takes it, fires it once, and is terrified that he may have hit a cat. Struggling with his guilt, he tells one lie after another until he cannot bear it anymore and must confess to someone.

Like Jake and Me   Mavis Jukes   Illustrated by Lloyd Bloom   Knopf

Alex wants to be liked by his rugged cowboy stepfather, but there are still barriers between the two. When Alex notices a wolf spider on Jake's neck and calmly mentions it, the rugged cowboy totally panics, admitting his terror of spiders. Alex comes to the rescue, and the two finally come to appreciate each other and their differences.

1984 AWARD

Dear Mr. Henshaw   Beverly Cleary
Illustrated by Paul O. Zelinsky   Morrow

Leigh Botts starts writing to the author of *Ways to Amuse a Dog* in second grade. Year after year the letters, and then a diary, become vehicles for expressing his feelings about himself, his parents' divorce, and his problems in school. Leigh's growth and acceptance of the divorce are tempered with much humor.

HONORS

The Wish Giver: Three Tales of Coven Tree   Bill Brittain
Illustrated by Andrew Glass   Harper & Row

Thaddeus Blinn, the wish giver, sells Polly, Rowena, Henry, and Stew Meat wishes. All they have to do is hold the white card with the dot and wish carefully. The first three make their wishes with dire but comical consequences and leave Stew Meat to use his to undo everything they have done.

Sugaring Time   Kathryn Lasky
Photographs by Christopher G. Knight   Macmillan

The author and photographer record a family's old-fashioned method of sugaring. When the right time finally comes, family members tap the maple trees, boil the sap, and enjoy a sugar-on-snow party and a pancake breakfast. The family's enjoyment of sugaring is evident in the often poetic text and the clear black-and-white photographs.

The Sign of the Beaver   Elizabeth George Speare   Houghton

Left alone in the Maine wilderness, Matt first loses his rifle and food and then is savagely stung by bees. Found by Saknis, chief of the Beaver tribe, Matt is cared for in exchange for teaching the chief's grandson to read. As the boys' friendship develops, Matt gains an appreciation for the heritage and skills of the Beaver tribe.

A Solitary Blue   Cynthia Voigt   Atheneum

Abandoned at the age of seven by his cause-conscious mother, Jeff is left to fend for himself and take care of his absent-minded-professor father. Not until Jeff is stricken with pneumonia at the age of twelve does his father understand how he, too, has deserted his son. Slowly the two build a close, strong relationship that is able to help them survive and grow.

1983 AWARD

Dicey's Song   Cynthia Voigt   Atheneum

Finally settled in with Gram Tillerman while their mother is in a mental hospital, Dicey and her brothers and sisters discover that it is not easy to become a family. They must learn to love and trust Gram—and she them—while they try to adjust to a new school and make friends.

HONORS

Graven Images: Three Stories   Paul Fleischman
Illustrated by Andrew Glass   Harper & Row

Three gripping stories, two sinister and one funny and all with historical settings, are centered on graven images: a wooden boy with a frightening secret, a weather-vane that leads to true love, and a statue ordered by a ghost.

Homesick: My Own Story   Jean Fritz   Illustrated by Margot Tomes
and with photographs   Putnam

Fritz remembers with humor and poignancy two years of her childhood in China during the turbulent 1920s. She contends with being a "foreign devil," losing a longed-for baby sister, and, most of all, longing for the United States, a country she has never seen.

Sweet Whispers, Brother Rush   Virginia Hamilton   Philomel

Life changes radically for fourteen-year-old Tree and her older retarded brother when the ghost of Brother Rush appears to Tree, first in the street and then in her home. The handsome ghost of her mother's brother takes her back in time to bear witness to the past and to learn about the terrible disease that is killing her own brother.

The Blue Sword   Robin McKinley   Greenwillow

Angharad Crewe is yanked out of an easy life on a Homelander outpost and thrust into one of rigorous training for her prophesied role as deliverer of the Hillfolk. She earns the right to carry the Blue Sword into battle, and with it she heroically leads a small band of warriors against the nonhuman Northerners.

Doctor De Soto   William Steig   Illustrated by the author   Farrar Straus Giroux

As mice dentists, the diminutive De Sotos have always refused to treat dangerous animals until a miserable fox appears begging for help. The compassionate mice cleverly find a way to rid the fox of his pain while guaranteeing their own safety.

1982 AWARD

A Visit to William Blake's Inn: Poems for Innocent and Experienced Travelers   Nancy Willard
Illustrated by Alice and Martin Provensen   Harcourt Brace Jovanovich

Written in the spirit of William Blake, these magical poems are built around the visit of a child to Blake's inn. It is staffed by mighty dragons that brew and bake, angels that wash feather beds, and animals that dance to the music of the Marmalade Man.

HONORS

Ramona Quimby, Age 8   Beverly Cleary
Illustrated by Alan Tiegreen   Morrow

Ramona is now starting the third grade and her life is full of the usual hilarious trials that cause her to be labeled a "nuisance and show-off" by her new teacher. Whether she is deciding she prefers her printed Q to the floppy cursive one, getting raw egg in her hair, or facing an interminably boring Sunday, Ramona is always a memorable character.

Upon the Head of the Goat: A Childhood in Hungary 1939–1944
Aranka Siegal   Farrar Straus Giroux

The destruction of nine-year-old Piri's family begins with Hungary's occupation by the Nazis. Her mother valiantly tries to keep the family together and safe, but one loss after another occurs until they board trains that will take them to Auschwitz. Siegal's book is a powerful autobiography.

1981 AWARD

Jacob Have I Loved   Katherine Paterson   Crowell

Although she takes pride in her twin sister's singing talent, Wheeze (Louise) is jealous of the attention Caroline gets on their Chesapeake Bay island. It is only when she leaves and starts a life as a midwife in Kentucky that Wheeze comes to understand that she has always been loved and accepted for herself.

HONORS

The Fledgling   Jane Langton   Illustrated by Erik Blegvad   Harper & Row

> Frail young Georgie, almost light enough to blow away, is obsessed with her belief that she can fly. When a large Canada goose she has befriended hoots outside her window, Georgie hops on his back and flies away. Night after night they soar above Walden Pond until one misfortune and then another end Georgie's flying forever.

A Ring of Endless Light   Madeleine L'Engle   Farrar Straus Giroux

> Sixteen-year-old Vicky and her family spend the summer on a New England island with her dying grandfather. All summer long she and her family are preoccupied with the mysteries of life, death, and eternity, yet there is still time for Vicky to help with a Marine Biology Station dolphin project and to date two boys.

1980 AWARD

A Gathering of Days: A New England Girl's Journal, 1830–32
Joan W. Blos   Scribner

Catherine Cabot Hall sporadically writes in her journal, filling it with recipes, excerpts from her copy book, secrets, fears, confidences, details of her adjustment to her stepmother, and thoughts on the pain of a friend's death. Though fiction, the journal is believable, and Catherine is easy to like.

HONOR

The Road from Home: The Story of an Armenian Girl
David Kherdian   Greenwillow

> After the Turks finish with their slaughter of nearly two million Armenians, Veron is the only survivor of her immediate family. When the Greeks attack Turkey, Veron and her aunt and cousin escape to Greece, and from there she travels to the United States, a mail-order bride and the future mother of the author.

1979 AWARD

The Westing Game   Ellen Raskin   Dutton

An expensive apartment building mysteriously fills up with sixteen occupants—all named as heirs or possible murderers in millionaire Sam Westing's will. The sixteen are paired, given $10,000, and challenged to discover who really killed Sam Westing.

HONOR

The Great Gilly Hopkins   Katherine Paterson   Crowell

Abandoned as a preschooler, Gilly has gone through a succession of foster homes. Smart, self-sufficient, and superficially hard, Gilly manages to do just what she wants until she is sent to stay with Maime Trotter, a woman with a big heart, patience, and wisdom enough to know how to reach the unhappy girl.

1978 AWARD

Bridge to Terabithia   Katherine Paterson
Illustrated by Donna Diamond   Crowell

After practicing all summer to be the fastest runner in school, Jess is beaten by the new girl, Leslie. Gradually the two become close friends, creating an imaginary world in the woods and calling it Terabithia. When tragedy strikes, Jess, shocked and despairing, slowly begins to see the wonders Leslie left him.

HONORS

Ramona and Her Father   Beverly Cleary
Illustrated by Alan Tiegreen   Morrow

Ramona is in second grade when her father loses his job and her mother begins to work full-time. Ramona tries her best to help her family through the crisis, even starting a campaign to get her father to quit smoking. Her worries, problems, and joys, presented with lively good humor, are common to many children her age.

Anpao: An American Indian Odyssey   Jamake Highwater
Illustrated by Fritz Scholder   Lippincott

A beautiful Indian maiden promises to marry Anpao, but first he must get the Sun's permission and have him remove the ugly scar on his face. As Anpao travels the world looking for the Sun, he hears stories about his own roots as well as legends and myths of his people.

1977 AWARD

Roll of Thunder, Hear My Cry   Mildred D. Taylor
Frontispiece by Jerry Pinkney   Dial

Cassie Logan and her brothers are part of a warm, intelligent, and courageous black family in rural Mississippi during the Depression. They try to maintain their pride as they take abuse from white children and then recognize that their personal difficulties are only symptoms of greater problems within their community.

HONORS

A String in the Harp   Nancy Bond   Margaret K. McElderry/Atheneum

> Their father's remoteness and the strangeness of school in Wales make the children's adjustment to their mother's death even more difficult. Then twelve-year-old Peter finds an ancient harp key that pulls him back into Welsh history, helping him discover a purpose to living.

Abel's Island   William Steig   Illustrated by the author   Farrar Straus Giroux

> After a violent storm, Abel, a mouse, finds himself alone, bewildered, and far, far away from his beloved wife Amanda. Sustained by his love for his wife, Abel uses all his resources to survive for a year on the deserted island.

1976 AWARD

> *The Grey King*   Susan Cooper
> Illustrated by Michael Heslop   Margaret K. McElderry/Atheneum

In Wales recovering from a serious illness, eleven-year-old Will, the youngest of the Old Ones, uses his considerable powers to find the golden harp that will awaken the Sleepers. It is not an easy quest, and Will has only the mysterious Bran and Bran's dog, Cafall, to help him fight the forces of dark and evil.

HONORS

The Hundred Penny Box   Sharon Bell Mathis
Illustrated by Leo and Diane Dillon   Viking

> For each of her hundred years there is a penny in Aunt Dew's box and a story to go along with it. More than his parents, Michael understands the importance of the box to the old woman and loves to hear her tell the stories again and again.

Dragonwings   Laurence Yep   Harper & Row

> In 1903 Moonshadow leaves the Middle Kingdom to join his father in San Francisco. To make the father's dream of building an aeroplane come true, the two of them leave the close-knit community that shelters their Chinese culture to live among white demons. Humorous accommodations are made between the different cultures as they grow in understanding and friendship.

1975 AWARD

> *M. C. Higgins, the Great*   Virginia Hamilton   Macmillan

Up on Sarah's Mountain, M. C. dreams of a way for his family to escape the spoil heap that may one day destroy their home. It is not his dreams but the boy's own strength and determination that help the family find a way to keep themselves safe.

HONORS

My Brother Sam Is Dead   James Lincoln Collier and
Christopher Collier   Four Winds

> Tim's older brother, Sam, defies their father and runs off to join the Continental Army. When their father is imprisoned by the rebels and dies and Sam is hung by his own army, Tim sees how devastating war can be.

Philip Hall Likes Me, I Reckon Maybe   Bette Greene
Illustrated by Charles Lilly   Dial

> Eleven-year-old Beth Lambert, a spunky heroine, realizes she has been letting Philip Hall be number one in school because she is afraid he will not like her if she surpasses him. With gentle prodding from her family, Beth decides to go ahead and do her best—even if it means beating Philip Hall.

The Perilous Gard   Elizabeth Marie Pope
Illustrated by Richard Cuffari   Houghton

> Banished by Queen Mary to the remote castle of Elvenwood, Kate Sutton quickly learns the castle's secret: It guards the last practitioners of the old religions. To keep their power, the fairy folk decide to sacrifice the man Kate loves on All Hallow's Eve.

Figgs & Phantoms   Ellen Raskin   Dutton

> Mona is embarrassed by her zany, ex-show business family—except for her four-foot-four-inch-tall Uncle Florence Italy Figg. When he dies, Mona is desolate. She is sure he has gone to Capri, the Figg family Heaven, and decides to follow him.

1974 AWARD

The Slave Dancer   Paula Fox   Illustrated by Eros Keith   Bradbury

Kidnapped and forced to play his fife while the slaves "dance," thirteen-year-old Jessie learns all too soon about the savagery of the slave trade. For four long months he lives with the crew's cruelty until a storm wrecks the ship and Jessie and Ras, a would-be slave, are the only survivors.

HONOR

The Dark Is Rising   Susan Cooper
Illustrated by Alan E. Cober   Margaret K. McElderry/Atheneum

> On midwinter's eve, Will's eleventh birthday, the world is in turmoil with strange creatures appearing and stranger things happening. Will, the last of the Old Ones to be born, must use all his knowledge and skill to help in the fight against the Dark.

1973 AWARD

Julie of the Wolves   Jean Craighead George
Illustrated by John Schoenherr   Harper & Row

Having run away from a forced marriage, thirteen-year-old Miyax, an Eskimo, becomes lost on the Arctic plain. Her only hope for survival is acceptance by a wolf pack. Imitating their facial expressions and body movements, Miyax slowly becomes one of them, while still trying to get to safety.

HONORS

Frog and Toad Together   Arnold Lobel   Illustrated by the author   Harper & Row

Whether they are testing their willpower with a bowl of cookies or their patience while waiting for seeds to grow, Frog and Toad delight in each other's company. Witty, easy-to-read, and full of warmth and gentle humor, these five stories engagingly explore the meaning of friendship.

The Upstairs Room   Johanna Reiss   Crowell

As the German occupation of Holland tightens, two Jewish sisters are forced to hide in a secret upstairs room in an old farmhouse for two years. The girls experience fear, hope, terror, and boredom in their daily life and depend on the kindness and courage of others for their survival.

The Witches of Worm   Zilpha Keatley Snyder
Illustrated by Alton Raible   Atheneum

Deserted by her friends and her mother, Jessica channels her anger at life into "evil acts" that her cat, Worm, supposedly forces her to perform. Convinced first that Worm is a witch's cat, then that she is a witch, Jessica is ultimately forced to face herself and her feelings.

1972 AWARD

Mrs. Frisby and the Rats of NIMH   Robert C. O'Brien,
pseud. (Robert Leslie Conly)   Illustrated by Zena Bernstein   Atheneum

When nothing she does seems to help her son Timothy get well, Mrs. Frisby, a widowed mouse, turns to a colony of super-intelligent rats for help. The rats' high intelligence is the result of experiments performed upon them by human scientists at NIMH. Now the rats are intent upon starting a new civilization free from human interference.

HONORS

Incident at Hawk's Hill   Allan W. Eckert
Illustrated by John Schoenherr   Little, Brown

> Lonely, small, and frail, six-year-old Ben shies away from people but shows deep interest in and affinity toward animals. Lost during a storm, he takes refuge with a badger who has just lost her young. The badger adopts him, and he lives a feral life for three months until he is found. Convincingly written, the incident is based on an actual occurrence in 1870.

The Planet of Junior Brown   Virginia Hamilton   Macmillan

> For more than two months, huge, musical genius Junior Brown and his friend and protector Buddy Clark have been cutting classes and hiding in a secret basement room created by the school custodian. Buddy and Mr. Poole, the custodian, are trying desperately to help Junior, who seems to be slipping slowly but inexorably into madness.

The Tombs of Atuan   Ursula K. LeGuin
Illustrated by Gail Garraty   Atheneum

> From the time Tenar was five, her life has been focused on the tombs and her future as their priestess. Renamed Arha, she guards the labyrinthine tunnels, knowing that they hide great treasure. When she finds a man (Ged of *A Wizard of Earthsea*) in the tunnels seeking the other half to the Ring of Erreth-Akbe, Arha is torn between her duty to kill him and her compassion for him.

Annie and the Old One   Miska Miles
Illustrated by Peter Parnall   Little, Brown

> Annie likes her life the way it is with her mother weaving, her father making jewelry, and her grandmother, the Old One, always there to tell her stories and to help with chores. When grandmother announces that she will die when the new rug is finished, Annie tries desperately to stop the inevitable by secretly unraveling the rug.

The Headless Cupid   Zilpha Keatley Snyder
Illustrated by Alton Raible   Atheneum

> Eleven-year-old David is pleased about his father's remarriage until he meets his new stepsister, Amanda, a self-proclaimed witch. Angry at her mother for remarrying, Amanda sets up situations that lead the other children to believe their house is haunted. Then unexplained events turn the tables, frightening even Amanda.

1971 AWARD

The Summer of the Swans   Betsy Byars
Illustrated by Ted CoConis   Viking

An insecure fourteen-year-old, Sarah is unhappy with herself and her family. Though she loves her mentally disabled brother Charlie, Sarah is tired of always being responsible for him. When Charlie turns up missing, however, Sarah tries desperately to find him and in the process discovers that she is less the ugly duckling than she had supposed.

HONORS

Knee Knock Rise   Natalie Babbitt   Farrar Straus Giroux

In this tale filled with folk humor, Egan goes to the village for a visit and becomes intrigued with the tales and wails of a monster that lives in the peaks of Knee Knock Rise. After an unprecedented climb up the mountain, Egan discovers the practical explanation for the legendary creature. The villagers refuse to listen to him, preferring to let their folklore live on as history.

Enchantress from the Stars   Sylvia Louise Engdahl
Illustrated by Rodney Shackell   Atheneum

Invaded by technologically advanced Imperials, the Andrecians are close to being destroyed by their occupiers when beings from an even more highly advanced civilization decide to intervene secretly. Using their telekenetic powers, three Federation members pose as magicians, teaching a young Andrecian how to use his psychic abilities to combat the invaders.

Sing Down the Moon   Scott O'Dell   Houghton

At fourteen, Bright Morning dares to be optimistic about her future. Her mother is a wealthy Navajo, and Bright Morning is to marry Tall Boy, a young Navajo warrior. Then she is wrenched from her home by Spanish slavers. When freed, she is uprooted again, this time by the cavalry, who force the Navajo to make a 300-mile march to Bosque Redondo.

1970 AWARD

Sounder   William H. Armstrong   Illustrated by James Barkley
Harper & Row

Sounder, the family dog, valiantly defends the father when the sheriff and his deputies come to arrest him for stealing food for his starving family. Years later, the dog, shot and maimed by the deputies, is the only one to recognize the father when he returns, paralyzed and deformed.

HONORS

Our Eddie   Sulamith Ish-Kishor   Pantheon

> Eddie's father is a stern, insensitive zealot who refuses, until it is too late, to see that his son is gradually succumbing to a debilitating disease. Set in London and New York in the 1920s, most of this story of a warm Jewish immigrant family is told by Eddie's insightful sister.

The Many Ways of Seeing: An Introduction to the Pleasures of Art
Janet Gaylord Moore   Illustrated with black-and-white and
color reproductions and photographs   World

> Moore, of the Cleveland Museum of Art, encourages readers to try a new way of approaching art: to see art reflecting the world and nature, and the world in turn reflecting art. Paintings (reproduced in color), poems, and quotations are arranged to lead to the discovery of new comparisons between modern, traditional, or ancient art and the imagery of word and picture.

Journey Outside   Mary Q. Steele   Illustrated by Rocco Negri   Viking

> In a story filled with allegory and symbolism, Dilar's people endlessly travel an underground river, headed for the "better place." But Dilar, suspecting that they are merely going around in circles, jumps from his raft and accidentally makes his way into the outside world. There, nearly blinded by the light, he tries to learn more about his people and to find a way to bring them aboveground.

1969 AWARD

The High King   Lloyd Alexander   Holt Rinehart & Winston

In the final book of the chronicles of Prydain, Taran leads his forces against Arawn and his army of the dead. Victorious, but with great loss of life and destruction to Prydain, Taran becomes High King, fulfilling the predictions of his wizard guardian, Dallben.

HONORS

To Be a Slave   Julius Lester   Illustrated by Tom Feelings   Dial

> American slaves, runaways, and emancipated people provide a powerful testament of how they felt about slavery and what they endured. The author dynamically blends quotations from published and unpublished sources and presents them in rough chronological order.

When Shlemiel Went to Warsaw and Other Stories   Isaac Bashevis Singer
Illustrated by Margot Zemach   Farrar Straus Giroux

> In eight delightfully silly stories, five retold from the Yiddish and three original, readers are introduced to a memorable collection of characters. Among them are a mixed-up Shlemiel, who does not recognize his wife and village, and Utzel's daughter, Poverty, who seems to grow larger as he grows poorer.

1968 AWARD

From the Mixed-Up Files of Mrs. Basil E. Frankweiler
E. L. Konigsburg   Illustrated by the author   Atheneum

Having carefully planned how and to where they will run away, Claudia and her little brother, James (and his money), board a bus, head to New York City, and go to the Metropolitan Museum of Art. There they hide in washrooms, sleep on ancient beds, and get involved in solving an exciting mystery.

HONORS

Jennifer, Hecate, Macbeth, William McKinley, and Me, Elizabeth
E. L. Konigsburg   Illustrated by the author   Atheneum

> Elizabeth is lonely at her new school until she meets Jennifer, a girl her age who claims to be a real witch. In awe of Jennifer, Elizabeth agrees to become her apprentice and initially finds her boring life full of adventure. But Jennifer is very demanding, and even superficially docile Elizabeth can only be pushed so far.

The Black Pearl   Scott O'Dell
Illustrated by Milton Johnson   Houghton

> In this story written with stark simplicity and riveting suspense, Ramon confronts his two greatest enemies in the waters of Baja California. The legendary curse of the Manta Diablo holds true when Ramon wrests the fabulous black pearl from the Manta's cave and his life is changed forever.

The Fearsome Inn   Isaac Bashevis Singer
Illustrated by Nonny Hogrogian   Scribner

> Unaware that the owners of the inn are a witch and her half-devil husband, three young men seek shelter there on a stormy winter night. One of the three, a clever student of the Cabala, recognizes the couple's evil and courageously defeats them, sending the pair "behind the Mountains of Darkness where there is neither day nor night."

The Egypt Game   Zilpha Keatley Snyder
Illustrated by Alton Raible   Atheneum

> April and Melanie begin the Egypt game in the backyard of a slightly sinister curio shop. With costumes, ceremonies, an evil god, an oracular owl, and four other members, the game is seriously and imaginatively played. After the murder of a child, they are forced inside for awhile, but finally they begin the game again. This time one of the players almost becomes the next victim.

1967 AWARD

Up a Road Slowly   Irene Hunt
Cover painting by Don Bolognese   Follett

When Julie is seven, her mother dies. She and her little brother are sent to live with her strict, schoolteacher aunt. Through the years, Julie keeps hoping that her father will want them back, that staying with Aunt Cordelia is just temporary, but slowly she comes to love her aunt and wants to stay.

HONORS

The King's Fifth   Scott O'Dell
Illustrated by Samuel Bryant   Houghton

> Imprisoned in Vera Cruz and awaiting trial, seventeen-year-old Esteban tells of his part in the disastrous expedition for gold to the Seven Cities of Cibola. A map-maker, Esteban is left with the bags of gold. After seeing the greed, cruelty, and, finally, death of those searching for it, he throws the gold into a volcanic crater.

Zlateh the Goat and Other Stories   Isaac Bashevis Singer
Illustrated by Maurice Sendak   Translated from the Yiddish
by the author and Elizabeth Shub   Harper & Row

> Seven stories rich with eastern European culture and Jewish folklore are filled with lively characters, delightfully funny fools, clever people, and loyal animals. The ink drawings of Sendak create wonderful scenes complementing the stories perfectly.

The Jazz Man   Mary Hays Weik   Illustrated by Ann Grifalconi   Atheneum

> Night after night Zeke and his mother and father listen to the jazz man play his piano. Then his mother tires of his father not working, and she leaves them. Soon his father goes as well, and Zeke is alone. As the gloomy days and nights pass, Zeke dreams of the jazz man and of better, happier times.

1966 AWARD

I, Juan de Pareja   Elizabeth Borton de Treviño   Farrar Straus Giroux

Behind the great painter Velasquez stands his faithful slave, Juan, ready to prepare a canvas, mix paint, and boost his morale. But, secretly, Juan teaches himself to paint, winning his freedom and the respect of a great master.

HONORS

The Black Cauldron   Lloyd Alexander   Henry Holt

Assistant Pig-Keeper Taran excitedly joins Gwydion and the other men of Prydain in their attack on Arawn, Lord of Annuvin, and his cauldron-born army. Only by destroying the cauldron can they hope to stop Arawn and his deathless warriors from overrunning Prydain.

The Animal Family   Randall Jarrell   Illustrated by Maurice Sendak   Pantheon

Isolated in his house by the sea, the hunter is lonely until the day he sees the mermaid. Together they form an amazing family with first a bear cub, then a lynx, and finally an orphaned boy. Each fits gently and beautifully into the very special world created by the unusual couple.

The Noonday Friends   Mary Stolz   Illustrated by Louis Glanzman
Harper & Row

Her hard-working mother and out-of-work father depend on Franny to take care of her little brother after school and to help out in other ways. The only time left for friendship is during lunch hour at school when she talks to Simone, a friend with whom she can share problems.

1965 AWARD

Shadow of a Bull   Maia Wojciechowska
Illustrated by Alvin Smith   Atheneum

With everyone waiting for him to become a great bullfighter like his father, Manolo is afraid to let them know that he has a different dream—to become a doctor. He trains and practices for the ring until finally he has the courage and confidence to admit that he can never be a bullfighter.

HONOR

Across Five Aprils   Irene Hunt   Follett

At nine, Jethro is excited by the prospect of a civil war coming to the country. When the nation really does go to war, his brothers and friends go in different directions, fighting for either the North or the South. Jethro begins to understand how devastating war really is to family and nation.

1964 AWARD

It's Like This, Cat Emily Neville
Illustrated by Emil Weiss Harper & Row

When his father suggests that owning a dog might be good for him, fourteen-year-old Dave defiantly goes to Aunt Kate the Cat Woman and adopts a stray. The cat ends up leading him to new people and adventures all over Manhattan—and even to an appreciation for his parents.

HONORS

Rascal: A Memoir of a Better Era Sterling North
Illustrated by John Schoenherr Dutton

> For twelve months Sterling owned the raccoon, raising him from a tiny captured kit to a large adult yearning for his freedom. Bright, curious, energetic, and endearing, Rascal fills the boy's life with love, companionship, and adventure during their year together.

The Loner Ester Wier Illustrated by Christine Price McKay

> Both nameless and homeless, the boy wanders the country with other migrants, hoping to find work and food. Finally, lost and weak from hunger, he collapses and is found by a woman called The Boss. The gruff but gentle sheep rancher names him David and gives him a chance to make his own life on her Montana ranch.

1963 AWARD

A Wrinkle in Time Madeleine L'Engle Ariel/Farrar Straus Giroux

Meg, Charles Wallace, and next-door neighbor Calvin go into space and through time to rescue Meg's father, a scientist who disappeared while working on a secret project. The children's intergalactic search leads them to a confrontation with the forces of evil on the planet Camazotz, where conformity means survival.

HONORS

Thistle and Thyme: Tales and Legends from Scotland Sorche Nic Leodhas, pseud.
(Leclaire Alger) Illustrated by Evaline Ness Holt Rinehart & Winston

> Using her memories of stories told in her family, the author retells ten stories based on Scottish legends and folktales. Some are humorous, others mysterious and suspenseful, and all of them possess the rhythm of the Gaelic language.

Men of Athens   Olivia Coolidge   Illustrated by Milton Johnson   Houghton

The golden age of Greece comes to life through the men and women who lived during and immediately before and after that brief fifty-year period. The battles they waged to make Greece strong and free; the brilliance of the leading artists, philosophers, and statesmen; and the excitement of the time make exciting reading.

1962 AWARD

The Bronze Bow   Elizabeth George Speare   Houghton

At the death of his parents, Daniel swears vengeance against the Roman invaders. For five years he hides in the mountains of Galilee with a band of rebels but finally must return to care for his sister. He meets Jesus but refuses to accept his message of love, wanting revenge instead. Only when all seems nearly lost does he start to understand the power of love.

HONORS

Frontier Living   Edwin Tunis   Illustrated by the author   World

Beginning with the settlement of the Piedmont area in the early 1700s, nineteen distinct frontier movements take American settlers from the East Coast across the continent and through the nineteenth century. Details of daily life and carefully drawn pictures of the people and objects show what makes this era unique.

The Golden Goblet   Eloise Jarvis McGraw   Coward

Under the control of his cruel and unscrupulous half-brother, Gebu, Ranofer, a boy of ancient Egypt who lives in Thebes, is sent to work for a goldsmith. Slowly he discovers that Gebu is stealing gold objects from the Valley of the Tombs, and he must find a way to expose him.

Belling the Tiger   Mary Stolz   Illustrated by Beni Montresor   Harper

Asa and Rambo, the two smallest mice, are given the dubious honor of belling the cat. While getting the bell, the two accidentally get stuck on a ship and travel to a tropical island where they "bell" a tiger. Home again, the diminutive duo have the courage to demand a raise in status.

1961 AWARD

Island of the Blue Dolphins   Scott O'Dell   Houghton

Accidentally left behind when her tribe flees, Karana spends eighteen years alone on an island off the coast of California. Her courage and resourcefulness help her to survive and to fill her life with moments of beauty and happiness.

HONORS

America Moves Forward: A History for Peter   Gerald W. Johnson
Illustrated by Leonard Everett Fisher   Morrow

> From World War I to 1956, major events and important men of politics are evaluated and discussed for their impact on American life and history. The third and final volume in a work that offers a personalized look at American history, the book is illustrated with striking scratchboard pictures.

Old Ramon   Jack Schaefer   Illustrated by Harold West   Houghton

> Old Ramon teaches the boy as much as he can during the months they spend with the sheep in the mountains. Along the way, Ramon shares stories of his youth as a shepherd with the boy's grandfather and brings the boy back to the valley with a keener understanding and appreciation for the life of a shepherd.

The Cricket in Times Square   George Selden, pseud. (George Thompson)
Illustrated by Garth Williams   Farrar Straus Giroux

> Accidentally brought into a New York City subway station, Chester Cricket is found by Mario Bellini, the son of a newsstand owner. Chester is befriended by two subway animals, Harry Cat and Tucker Mouse, who encourage him to use his musical talents to help the Bellinis. An overnight success, Chester nonetheless longs to return to the country.

1960 AWARD

Onion John   Joseph Krumgold   Illustrated by Symeon Shimin   Crowell

Twelve-year-old Andy is torn between his love for his father and his affection for Onion John, the old man whose way of life is totally foreign to nearly everyone in town. When members of the Rotary Club try to build Onion John a new house, their actions have great repercussions.

HONORS

My Side of the Mountain   Jean Craighead George   Dutton

> Tired of living in a crowded city apartment, Sam Gribley runs away from home and heads for his Grandpa Gribley's long-lost homestead in the Catskill Mountains. For a year he stays alone, learning to live off the land, hollowing out a tree for a home, taming a falcon, and using every bit of ingenuity and resourcefulness he has to survive.

America Is Born: A History for Peter   Gerald W. Johnson
Illustrated by Leonard Everett Fisher   Morrow

> Johnson's account of America's history is a very personal retelling of the lives and adventures of the people who explored and settled this country. The first in a three-volume series, the book covers the time from Columbus to the Revolutionary War and the Constitutional Convention.

The Gammage Cup   Carol Kendall   Illustrated by Erik Blegvad   Harcourt

> Five misfits are sent into exile in the mountains when they refuse to conform to Minnepin traditions of dress, ideas, and lifestyle. They come to the rescue of the Land between the Mountains when they uncover an invasion plot by the Mushroom People.

1959 AWARD

The Witch of Blackbird Pond   Elizabeth George Speare   Houghton

When her grandfather dies, sixteen-year-old Kit leaves the West Indies to live with her Puritan Aunt Rachel and her family. Kit's lively personality, her bright clothes, and her friendship with an outcast Quaker woman make her a target for charges of witchcraft in 1687 New England.

HONORS

The Family under the Bridge   Natalie Savage Carlson
Illustrated by Garth Williams   Harper

> Armand, who wanders the streets of Paris without a care, finds that his place beneath a bridge has been invaded by three children and their mother. Though he does not want to have anything to do with the children, the old man soon becomes a grandfather figure to the family, helping them, sharing the fun of the city, and ultimately making them his responsibility.

Along Came a Dog   Meindert DeJong   Illustrated by Maurice Sendak
Harper & Row

> When her frostbitten toes fall off, the little red hen becomes a target for the other chickens' abuse. Only the big, homeless dog comes to her rescue, looking on her as something to guard and love as he tries to make the farm his home.

Chucaro: Wild Pony of the Pampa   Francis Kalnay
Illustrated by Julian de Miskey   Harcourt

> Once wild on the Argentine pampa, Chucaro is captured and tamed by Pedrito and his gaucho friend Juan. When the patron demands a gentle horse for his

spoiled and cruel son, it is Chucaro he gets in spite of Pedrito's determination to keep him.

The Perilous Road   William O. Steele   Illustrated by Paul Galdone   Harcourt

Eleven-year-old Chris passionately hates the Yankees invading his Tennessee homeland and wants to do anything to help the South. He is deaf to his father's words when he says war is the worst thing that can happen to people. Then Chris is caught in the middle of a savage battle and realizes how horrible war really is.

1958 AWARD

Rifles for Watie   Harold Keith   Crowell

Sixteen-year-old Jeff, already a combat veteran in the Union Army and winner of the Congressional Medal of Honor, is captured by the rebel troops of General Stand Watie, a Cherokee Indian, and forced to become one of his scouts.

HONORS

Gone-Away Lake   Elizabeth Enright
Illustrated by Beth and Joe Krush   Harcourt

All summer Julian and his ten-year-old cousin Portia explore the houses they discover around Gone-Away Lake. They tell no one about the place or the two old people living in one of the houses until a near tragedy exposes their secret.

Tom Paine, Freedom's Apostle   Leo Gurko   Illustrated by Fritz Kredel   Crowell

With hardly any education or money and only Ben Franklin's letter of introduction, Tom Paine goes to America and writes *Common Sense,* the first of his revolutionary pamphlets. The power and vision of Paine's writings and the violent feelings they aroused throughout his life are evident in this biography.

The Great Wheel   Robert Lawson   Viking

Aunt Honoria predicts that Conn will leave Ireland and head west. Now he is in Chicago working on a construction project for a man named Ferris. His aunt has also made the wild prediction that he will ride the world's biggest wheel. Conn does as soon as Mr. Ferris's daring project is completed for the Chicago World's Columbian Exposition of 1893.

The Horsecatcher   Mari Sandoz   Westminster

Unlike the other Cheyenne boys, Young Elk refuses to kill. He wants to capture and tame the wild horses of the prairie. When his father insists he join in their war, he runs away, returning months later with fifteen horses and the start of what becomes a nearly legendary way with wild horses.

1957 AWARD

Miracles on Maple Hill   Virginia Sorensen
Illustrated by Beth and Joe Krush   Harcourt Brace

When her father finally returns from being a prisoner of war, Marley's family decides to try to make a new beginning on a beautiful farm in Pennsylvania. During their first year there, they marvel at the miracle of the sap rising in the maple trees and the changes in each other.

HONORS

Black Fox of Lorne   Marguerite de Angeli   Doubleday

Shipwrecked off the coast of medieval Scotland, identical twins Jan and Brus are the only ones left alive when their father and his men are murdered. They survive by tricking the Scots into thinking that only one of them exists. Having sworn to avenge their father's murder, they foil the man's treasonous plot and keep their vow.

The House of Sixty Fathers   Meindert DeJong
Illustrated by Maurice Sendak   Harper

Alone in his family sampan, Tien Pao lands in Japanese-occupied China and begins a dangerous journey back to Hengyang during World War II. On his way, a company of American airmen adopt him, and he finds himself with sixty strange but kind fathers who help him find his family.

Old Yeller   Fred Gipson   Illustrated by Carl Burger   Harper

Left to help care for the homestead while his father takes their cattle to Kansas, fourteen-year-old Travis initially resents the intrusion of the big yellow dog. The dog proves his worth by rescuing little Arliss from a bear and Travis from wild hogs, guaranteeing himself a home.

Mr. Justice Holmes   Clara Ingram Judson
Illustrated by Robert Todd   Follett

The son of a famous writer, Oliver Wendell Holmes Jr. is a daydreamer whose brilliance is not always apparent to his family. After serving in the Civil War, he becomes a lawyer and a teacher, trying to make law interesting and clear to those entering the profession. Well-respected but never wealthy, he becomes one of the country's most highly esteemed Supreme Court justices.

The Corn Grows Ripe   Dorothy Rhoads   Illustrated by Jean Charlot   Viking

A happy but often irresponsible twelve-year-old Yucatan boy must suddenly grow up when his father is injured. Tigre bravely goes to another village to get a bonesetter and then sets about clearing and burning the family's new corn field, a ritualized duty that goes back to Mayan times. He proves he can be reliable.

1956 AWARD

Carry On, Mr. Bowditch   Jean Lee Latham
Illustrated by John O'Hara Cosgrave II   Houghton

In spite of having little education, Nat Bowditch manages to teach himself mathematics and the principles of navigation. When he gets the chance to sail as a second mate, he teaches the rest of the crew to navigate and even finds mistakes in the navigational tables. He later rewrites the tables, and they become a standard navigational tool.

HONORS

The Golden Name Day   Jennie Lindquist
Illustrated by Garth Williams   Harper

Staying with her Swedish-American grandparents while her mother is hospitalized, Nancy is warmly welcomed into an extended family of aunts, uncles, and cousins. With everyone else having a special Swedish Name Day to celebrate, the family unsuccessfully tries to find a matching Swedish name for Nancy. Only when a new family moves in is Nancy's problem solved.

The Secret River   Marjorie Kinnan Rawlings
Illustrated by Leonard Weisgard   Scribner

When hard times come to the Florida forest people, little Calpurnia and her dog, Buggyhorse, go to the wise woman of the forest for help. Advised to follow her nose, Calpurnia discovers a beautiful river full of fish. She catches many and brings them home, making hard times "soft."

Men, Microscopes, and Living Things   Katherine Shippen
Illustrated by Anthony Ravielli   Viking

The author begins with Aristotle and his investigation of natural science, then moves on to Pliny, Harvey, Linnaeus, Lamarck, and others. The lively yet factual writing provides interesting insights into the work of significant biologists.

1955 AWARD

The Wheel on the School   Meindert DeJong
Illustrated by Maurice Sendak   Harper

Inspired by Lina's composition about storks, her classmates and teacher decide to find a way to bring the birds and their luck back to their little Dutch village. As the children involve the people of the village in the search for a wheel and for a way to attach it to their school, they bring their small community together.

HONORS

The Courage of Sarah Noble   Alice Dalgliesh
Illustrated by Leonard Weisgard   Scribner

"Keep up your courage," Sarah's mother tells her when she leaves with her father to build a home in the wilderness. The home finished, Sarah stays with friendly Indians while her father goes back for the rest of the family.

Banner in the Sky: The Story of a Boy and a Mountain
James Ullman   Lippincott

Although his father died trying to climb the Citadel, the highest mountain in the Alps, Rudy is determined to scale it himself. He hides his climbing ability from his mother and his Alpine-guide uncle and joins an English expedition hoping to be able to plant his father's red shirt at the top as a banner in the sky.

1954 AWARD

. . . And Now Miguel   Joseph Krumgold
Illustrated by Jean Charlot   Crowell

Every spring Miguel hopes this is the year he will be asked to join the men as they take their sheep up into the Sangre de Cristo Mountains of New Mexico. When at the age of twelve he is told it is not yet time for him, he works hard and prays that his father will see how grown up he is.

HONORS

All Alone   Claire Huchet Bishop
Illustrated by Feodor Rojankovsky   Viking

When his father sends him to the high pastures with the heifers, Marcel is force-fully reminded of the village motto, "Each man for himself." But loneliness makes the yodel of another boy welcome, and when disaster strikes, Marcel is saved by his willingness to help someone else.

Magic Maize   Mary and Conrad Buff   Illustrated by the authors   Houghton

With the gringo world encroaching on the old ways of the Indians of Guatemala, a father continues to teach his son the old ways of farming and of praying to the gods of planting and harvest. Yet when their crop fails, it is the gringos who come to the family's aid.

Hurry Home, Candy   Meindert DeJong   Illustrated by Maurice Sendak   Harper

Taken from his mother before he is weaned and given to a family that only knows how to hurt and control him, Candy is lost on a family outing and becomes a stray. He longs for his own home and for people who will really love him.

Shadrach   Meindert DeJong   Illustrated by Maurice Sendak   Harper

After Davie's grandfather promises him a rabbit of his own, the little boy's excitement is nearly uncontainable. Davie bravely gathers food near a dangerous Dutch canal, helps get his hutch ready, and, when the rabbit arrives, lavishes attention and affection on the little animal.

Theodore Roosevelt, Fighting Patriot   Clara Ingram Judson
Illustrated by Lorence F. Bjorklund   Follett

Independent and honorable, Theodore is forever facing challenges because of his poor health, bad vision, and determination to learn as much as he can. As an adult he is remembered for leading the Rough Riders up San Juan Hill, starting our national park system, and being a president with tremendous courage and integrity.

1953 AWARD

Secret of the Andes   Ann Nolan Clark
Illustrated by Jean Charlot   Viking

Determined to discover another way of life, Cusi leaves his beautiful Incan home in the Andes Mountains and goes to the lowlands of Spanish Peru. Once there he longs for the hidden valley and the Old One. He returns knowing that he will never again willingly leave his home or break his vow to keep the Incan secret.

HONORS

The Bears on Hemlock Mountain   Alice Dalgliesh
Illustrated by Helen Sewell   Scribner

"There are no bears on Hemlock Mountain, no bears at all," Jonathan repeats as he goes over the mountain to borrow the big iron pot. But on the way back, Jonathan learns that there are indeed bears on Hemlock Mountain.

Birthdays of Freedom, Vol. I   Genevieve Foster
Illustrations by the author   Scribner

Starting with the excitement of the signing of the Declaration of Independence, the author sweeps back in time to the cave dwellers. From that time to the fall of Rome in 476 A.D., the determination to gain freedom is shown as the spark that encourages great inventions, discoveries, and political movements.

Moccasin Trail   Eloise Jarvis McGraw   Illustrated by Paul Galdone Coward

A runaway who is clawed by a grizzly and left for dead, Jim is raised by the Crow Indians and becomes a mountain man. Receiving a letter from his little brother asking for help, Jim finds his orphaned family on a wagon train heading to Oregon. He agrees to stay with them on the dangerous journey west. It is Jim's courage and Crow training that help them survive.

Red Sails to Capri   Ann Weil   Illustrated by C. B. Falls   Viking

Three wealthy strangers come to Michele's small island village and stay at his parents' inn. Their good spirits and desire for adventure soon convince Michele and his friends to help the strangers explore a forbidden cave. Their discovery of the now-famous Blue Grotto changes the lives of everyone on Capri.

Charlotte's Web   E. B. White   Illustrated by Garth Williams   Harper

After being raised by the farmer's daughter, Wilbur, a pig, is sold to another farm where his companion is a gray spider named Charlotte. When it becomes apparent that Wilbur is being fattened up for slaughtering, Charlotte promises to save him. The words that begin appearing in Charlotte's web amaze the farmer and bring hope to Wilbur.

1952 AWARD

Ginger Pye   Eleanor Estes   Illustrated by Louis Slobodkin
Harcourt Brace

The only clue to the mysterious disappearance of Ginger, the Pye family dog, is the unusual man in the mustard-colored hat. Jerry and Rachel look everywhere for their little dog, occasionally seeing the mustard-hatted man, and finally solve the mystery of Ginger's disappearance.

HONORS

Americans before Columbus   Elizabeth Baity   Illustrated by C. B. Falls   Viking

A study of pre-Columbian peoples in the Americas, this book describes their art, architecture, music, literature, and culture from the earliest times to that of Columbus. The text is prefaced with photographs of art and architecture and includes ink drawings in every chapter.

The Apple and the Arrow   Mary and Conrad Buff
Illustrated by the authors   Houghton

Caught by tyrant Gessler's soldier, Walter's father, William Tell, is forced to either shoot an apple on Walter's head or die. He successfully shoots the apple but is imprisoned. Breaking free, Tell kills Gessler and starts the revolution that wins Switzerland's freedom.

Minn of the Mississippi   Holling Clancy Holling   Houghton

Over a twenty-five-year period a snapping turtle makes her way from the source of the Mississippi to the Delta. Along the way she encounters a variety of adventures, lays eggs as she grows older, and introduces readers to the varied people, places, and wildlife along the river.

The Defender   Nicholas Kalashnikoff
Illustrated by Claire and George Louden   Scribner

In turn-of-the-century Siberia, Turgen, a widowed hunter and herbalist, becomes the target of the local shaman when he begins to protect the shy, fast-disappearing mountain rams. Turgen's only friends are a poor widow, whom he befriends and marries, and her two children.

The Light at Tern Rock   Julia L. Sauer   Illustrated by Georges Schreiber   Viking

Although Mr. Flagg has promised to get them back to shore by December 15, Aunt Martha and Ronnie suddenly realize that they are stuck at the lonely lighthouse until after Christmas. At first angry and sullen, Ronnie finally joins Aunt Martha in a very special celebration of the holiday.

1951 AWARD

Amos Fortune, Free Man   Elizabeth Yates
Illustrated by Nora S. Unwin   Aladdin/American Book

Captured by slavers, Amos, son of an African king, survives the long ocean voyage only to be sold to a New England Quaker. After years of serving and learning from others, Amos buys his own freedom, sets up his own business, and begins to buy and set free other slaves.

HONORS

Gandhi, Fighter without a Sword   Jeanette Eaton
Illustrated by Ralph Ray   Morrow

From an upper-class life in India, Gandhi travels to England where he becomes a lawyer. Later he goes to South Africa and becomes involved in fighting for civil liberties. Back in India, Gandhi spends the remainder of his life leading the non-violent independence movement, which finally brings freedom to India and martyrdom to Gandhi.

Better Known as Johnny Appleseed   Mabel Leigh Hunt
Illustrated by James Daugherty   Lippincott

> Loved by the settlers and the Indians, John Chapman carves a new name and legend for himself by trekking through the wilderness planting apple trees and helping anyone in need. The few facts known about Chapman are carefully interwoven with the Johnny Appleseed legends.

Abraham Lincoln, Friend of the People   Clara Ingram Judson
Illustrated with drawings by Robert Frankenberg and Kodachromes
of the Chicago Historical Society Lincoln Dioramas   Follett

> Vividly written and carefully researched, the book portrays the struggles Abraham Lincoln has in learning to read, making a living, and finally entering politics. The difficulties of life on the frontier and the problems leading to the Civil War form the background.

The Story of Appleby Capple   Anne Parrish   Illustrated by the author   Harper

> For his Cousin Clement's ninety-ninth birthday, five-year-old Appleby is determined to give the old man the thing he wants most to see: a zebra butterfly. The boy wanders through the alphabet looking for the butterfly. Ink illustrations work people and objects around all twenty-six letters.

1950 AWARD

The Door in the Wall   Marguerite de Angeli
Illustrated by the author   Doubleday

Crippled by a strange disease, Robin is ready to give up since he knows he will never be a knight. Then the monks help him to find ways to gain strength and courage and ultimately to play an important role in saving his medieval city.

HONORS

Tree of Freedom   Rebecca Caudill
Illustrated by Dorothy B. Morse   Viking

> During the American Revolution, the Venable family leaves North Carolina to seek new land and get away from British oppression. Their exciting month-long trek over the mountains to Kentucky starts them on the way to new freedom, symbolized by the apple tree, whose seeds have come with the family all the way from France.

The Blue Cat of Castle Town   Catherine Cate Coblentz
Illustrated by Janice Holland   Longmans, Green

> Born under a blue moon, the little kitten is destined to carry the river's song of beauty, peace, and contentment to the unhappy people of Castle Town, Vermont.

They have exchanged beauty for money, no longer making things with honesty and unable to "sing their own songs."

George Washington   Genevieve Foster   Illustrated by the author   Scribner

Filled with interesting excerpts from letters and diaries, this animated portrayal of the first president of the United States tells of George Washington's childhood and his many challenges as surveyor, soldier, commander in chief, and president.

Song of the Pines: A Story of Norwegian Lumbering in Wisconsin
Walter and Marion Havighurst   Illustrated by Richard Floethe   Winston

An orphan, fifteen-year-old Nils joins the Svendsen family and other Norwegian emigrants as they head toward America in the 1850s. They travel to Wisconsin where they stake out a claim for a farm. Nils, having found work in the lumber camps, creates his own business and future in America.

Kildee House   Rutherford Montgomery
Illustrated by Barbara Cooney   Doubleday

Not used to talking or being around people, Jerome Kildee retires to a small house he builds atop a hill in the redwood forest of northern California. Through the animals he shelters and the young people he meets, Kildee's life and the lives of those he encounters become fuller and richer than he ever imagined.

1949 AWARD

King of the Wind   Marguerite Henry
Illustrated by Wesley Dennis   Rand McNally

Sure that the motherless Arabian colt is going to be a great racer, Agba, the Sultan's mute slaveboy, raises the animal and stays with it, even when the horse is sent to France. Times are hard for the two, and they are often treated cruelly, but Agba never gives up his belief in the horse that becomes the ancestor of the great Man o' War.

HONORS

Story of the Negro   Arna Bontemps   Illustrated by Raymond Lufkin   Knopf

Beginning with the first slave ship to come to Jamestown, Bontemps celebrates the culture and accomplishments of black people throughout the world: from the cultural heritage of Africa to the artists, leaders, and momentous events that have shaped not only black but world culture as well.

My Father's Dragon   Ruth Stiles Gannett
Illustrated by Ruth Chrisman Gannett   Random House

An old alley cat convinces the narrator's father to rescue a baby dragon being used as a ferry by the animals of faraway Wild Island. With chewing gum, toothpaste, lollipops, and ribbons, the little boy keeps lions and tigers from eating him as he tries to rescue the little dragon.

Seabird   Holling Clancy Holling   Houghton

To help him while away the hours on the whaling ship, Ezra carves a mascot, Seabird, which becomes his constant companion as he journeys around the world and finally gets his own ship. For four generations Seabird brings companionship and luck to Ezra's family as they sail the sea.

Daughter of the Mountains   Louise Rankin
Illustrated by Kurt Wiese   Viking

When Momo's beloved Lhasa terrier is stolen by a wool trader, the Tibetan girl follows him on a long and dangerous journey that takes her through the mountains into India and finally to Calcutta.

1948 AWARD

The Twenty-One Balloons   William Pène du Bois
Illustrated by the author   Viking

Professor Sherman leaves San Francisco in one hot air balloon and three weeks later is found in the Atlantic Ocean, clinging to the remains of twenty balloons and refusing to tell how he got there.

HONORS

The Quaint and Curious Quest of Johnny Longfoot   Catherine Besterman
Illustrated by Warren Chappell   Bobbs-Merrill

Sent to the country to stay with his very thrifty uncle, Johnny, son of the shoe king, outwits guard dogs and a bear to reach the miserly old man. Not welcome, he goes on a quest that leads him to a cat who sends him to look for gold and seven-league boots. Leading a band of dogs, cats, bears, and his tagalong uncle, Johnny resourcefully succeeds in his mission.

Pancakes-Paris   Claire Huchet Bishop
Illustrated by Georges Schreiber   Viking

Before the war there was heat and food and paper. Now Charles wishes for a way to show his little sister the fun of Mardi Gras and the wonderful crepes they ate. When two American soldiers suddenly enter his life and give him a strange box that they claim holds the ingredients for crepes, things start to happen.

The Cow-tail Switch, and Other West African Stories   Harold Courlander
Illustrated by Madye Lee Chastain   Holt

> Puns, trickster tales, creation tales, parables, and proverbs form the basis for these
> seventeen stories from West Africa. Faithfully retold from original sources, the sto-
> ries are great fun to read or tell.

Li Lun, Lad of Courage   Carolyn Treffinger
Illustrated by Kurt Wiese   Abingdon

> When Li Lun refuses to join his father on his trip out to sea, the man angrily sends
> the boy up to the top of their mountain to grow rice. Alone on the mountaintop
> for 120 days, Li Lun, called a coward by his father and the other boys, courageously
> faces the elements, determined to complete his task.

Misty of Chincoteague   Marguerite Henry
Illustrated by Wesley Dennis   Rand McNally

> When Pony Penning Day comes on Chincoteague Island, Maureen and Paul are
> determined to buy the Phantom and her filly, Misty. They work hard and save
> $102, and finally the two spirited animals are theirs. Now the children must train
> the wild ponies to be around people, instead of running wild on Assateague.

1947 AWARD

Miss Hickory   Carolyn Sherwin Bailey
Illustrated by Ruth Gannett   Viking

With an apple twig for a body and a hickory nut for a head, Miss Hickory stubbornly
refuses help as she tries to survive a cold New Hampshire winter alone.

HONORS

Wonderful Year   Nancy Barnes, pseud. (Helen Simmons Adams)
Illustrated by Kate Seredy   Messner

> Eleven-year-old Ellen and her fun-loving parents move from an easy life in Kan-
> sas to a ranch in western Colorado. They enjoy life as they plant trees and build a
> home and a barn. For Ellen, the best part is her friendship with fifteen-year-old
> Ronnie and the adventures they share.

Big Tree   Mary and Conrad Buff   Illustrated by the authors   Viking

> A glorious tree that can live thousands of years and has no fear of fire or insects,
> the redwood Wawona begins to grow long before the pyramids and the coming
> of Christ. Nothing threatens the huge and ancient tree until man arrives with
> axes and saws. But others recognize his importance and offer protection to the
> redwood.

The Avion My Uncle Flew   Cyrus Fisher, pseud. (Darwin L. Teilhet)
Illustrated by Richard Floethe   Appleton

> When John's father returns home after World War II, he decides to take his wife and son to France. There John will have a chance to get his injured leg treated and to see his mother's homeland. John does not want to go, but he has no choice. Once there he becomes involved in a mysterious adventure that takes him to southern France and his glider-building uncle.

The Heavenly Tenants   William Maxwell   Illustrated by Ilonka Karasz   Harper

> The night before the Maxwells are to leave for three weeks in Virginia, father takes the children outside and shows them the different constellations that make up the zodiac. When no one comes to care for their animals while they are gone, the signs of the zodiac come to Earth and do it for them.

The Hidden Treasure of Glaston   Eleanore Jewett
Illustrated by Frederick T. Chapman   Viking

> When he is forced to leave the country because of his part in the murder of Thomas à Becket, Sir Hugh de Morville leaves his crippled son in the care of the monks at Glaston. As the boy and a new friend explore the area, they discover treasure left by King Arthur and his court and begin an exciting and suspenseful search for the Holy Grail.

1946 AWARD

Strawberry Girl   Lois Lenski   Illustrated by the author   Lippincott

Birdie's family wants to make a good living growing strawberries and oranges in turn-of-the-century Florida. Unfortunately their shiftless neighbors, the Slaters, fight them every step of the way.

HONORS

Justin Morgan Had a Horse   Marguerite Henry
Illustrated by Wesley Dennis   Rand McNally

> Justin Morgan does not want the little colt that follows him and Joel home. But Joel raises and trains it, and the two soon realize that the little horse is something very special, not to mention very fast. Years later it becomes the first of a new breed: the Justin Morgan horse.

The Moved-Outers   Florence Crannell Means
Illustrated by Helen Blair   Houghton

> After the attack on Pearl Harbor, the Ohara family, who have always thought of themselves as Americans, are suddenly "Japanese." Put into internment camps

with only the barest of necessities, Sue and her family try not only to survive but to stay loyal Americans.

New Found World   Katherine Shippen   Illustrated by C. B. Falls   Viking

A history of Latin America, the book begins with a chapter on the topography and the plant and animal life of the area. Additional chapters discuss the native peoples and their interaction with European explorers and colonists. Well-researched, the book covers aspects of Latin American life and history up to the end of World War II.

Bhimsa, the Dancing Bear   Christine Weston
Illustrated by Roger Duvoisin   Scribner

While aimlessly walking in his Indian garden, David is surprised by the approach of a boy, Gopala, and his tame bear, Bhimsa. He eagerly runs away with the two as they wander through India trying to find a way home for Gopala. Bhimsa's dancing attracts attention everywhere, earning them food and getting them into and out of trouble along the way.

1945 AWARD

Rabbit Hill   Robert Lawson   Illustrated by the author   Viking

The excitement among the wild creatures is contagious as Little Georgie enthusiastically tells every one of them that new folks are coming to the old farmhouse. All of the animals anxiously await the day the newcomers will arrive, afraid they might be the kind who have guns or dogs or even poison.

HONORS

The Silver Pencil   Alice Dalgliesh   Illustrated by Katherine Milhous   Scribner

After her father's sudden death, Janet and her mother begin a series of moves that take them from Trinidad, to England, to the United States, and then to Nova Scotia. Along the way, Janet holds fast to the silver pencil her father gave her, finding that writing is a solace.

Lone Journey: The Life of Roger Williams   Jeanette Eaton
Illustrated by Woodi Ishmael   Harcourt Brace

From childhood onward, Roger Williams is a champion for religious freedom. Again and again he speaks out for separation of church and state, risking his own life and trying to save the lives of others. Finally Williams becomes the founder of the Providence Colony in America, where settlers of all religious faiths can find refuge.

The Hundred Dresses   Eleanor Estes
Illustrated by Louis Slobodkin   Harcourt Brace

> Wanda Petronski, who speaks in broken English and always wears the same spar-
> kling clean dress to school each day, brags to the other girls that she has a hundred
> dresses at home. Wanda is laughed at and teased by the other girls, and she and her
> family move away. Only then do the girls find Wanda's beautifully drawn pictures
> of one hundred dresses.

Abraham Lincoln's World: 1809–1865   Genevieve Foster
Illustrated by the author   Scribner

> As Abraham Lincoln grows from birth to death, the things happening throughout
> the world affect him and his country. Chapter by chapter the stories of not only
> Lincoln but also Napolean, Jefferson, Tecumseh, Jackson, Bismarck, and others are
> told alternately to give a full and fascinating picture of world events.

1944 AWARD

Johnny Tremain: A Novel for Old and Young   Esther Forbes
Illustrated by Lynd Ward   Houghton

Fourteen-year-old apprentice silversmith Johnny Tremain has a terrible accident that
forces him to give up his work. He becomes involved with Sam Adams and the other
Boston patriots, takes part in the Boston Tea Party, and plays a role in the battle of
Lexington.

HONORS

Rufus M.   Eleanor Estes   Illustrated by Louis Slobodkin   Harcourt Brace

> A lively and imaginative little boy, Rufus is the youngest of the four Moffat chil-
> dren. Anxious to do his part for the war effort, he knits washcloths, plants a victory
> garden, and earns enough money selling popcorn to become a Victory Boy.

Fog Magic   Julia L. Sauer   Illustrated by Lynd Ward   Viking

> In every generation of Addingtons there is one person for whom the dense fog
> of Nova Scotia is magical. Walking toward the deserted village of Blue Cove on a
> foggy day, Greta comes upon a thriving village she has never seen before. It is the
> Blue Cove of one hundred years ago.

These Happy Golden Years   Laura Ingalls Wilder
Illustrated by Helen Sewell and Mildred Boyle   Harper

> Laura Ingalls, though still a student herself, begins teaching in small schools and
> sewing to earn tuition money for Mary's education. Whether working hard in

town, teaching, living on her family's claim on the Dakota prairie, or finally deciding to marry Almanzo, Laura realizes how lucky she is to have her warm, happy family.

Mountain Born Elizabeth Yates Illustrated by Nora S. Unwin Coward

Nursed back to life by Peter's mother, Biddy, a black lamb, is given to six-year-old Peter to raise. Bright and brave, Biddy becomes the leader of the herd, repeatedly alerting her human keepers to impending disaster.

1943 AWARD

Adam of the Road Elizabeth Janet Gray
Illustrated by Robert Lawson Viking

Adam, his minstrel father, their horse, and Adam's trained dog, Nick, are traveling in thirteenth-century England, singing and telling stories for food and a place to sleep. When Nick is stolen, father and son try desperately to find him and become separated from each other.

HONORS

The Middle Moffat Eleanor Estes
Illustrated by Louis Slobodkin Harcourt Brace

Janey is the "middle Moffat," trying hard to be serious and to do everything well. Things do not seem to work out quite as she plans (her organ recital turns into an escape for thousands of moths), but the little girl is undeterred. She continues to make bold plans with outrageously funny results.

"Have You Seen Tom Thumb?" Mabel Leigh Hunt
Illustrated by Fritz Eichenberg Lippincott

From the age of five, Charles Sherwood Stratton, only twenty-five inches tall and weighing fifteen pounds, is presented to the world by P. T. Barnum as General Tom Thumb. A charming, humorous person, he travels all over the world with Barnum.

1942 AWARD

The Matchlock Gun Walter Edmonds
Illustrated by Paul Lantz Dodd, Mead

Edward, his mother, and his little sister have only one defense against the French and the Indians—a huge matchlock gun. When attacked, his mother is wounded, and Edward must use the gun to save their lives.

HONORS

George Washington's World   Genevieve Foster
Illustrated by the author   Scribner

> From birth to death, the story of George Washington's life and the lives of other well-known kings, soldiers, politicians, and scientists of the same period are interwoven. In each section the author skillfully provides a worldview of events.

Down Ryton Water   Eva Roe Gaggin   Illustrated by Elmer Hader   Viking

> Escaping the religious persecution of their English countrymen, Matt and his family and neighbors head down Ryton Water for freedom in Holland. Finally ready to face the long and dangerous voyage to the New World, all of them board the Mayflower and Speedwell to sail to what becomes the Plymouth Colony.

Indian Captive: The Story of Mary Jemison   Lois Lenski
Illustrated by the author   Lippincott

> Even though other settlers have been slaughtered by the French and the Indians, Pa refuses to let his family go east to safety. They, too, are captured, and only young, blond-haired Mary survives, forced to become a part of the Seneca people.

Little Town on the Prairie   Laura Ingalls Wilder
Illustrated by Helen Sewell and Mildred Boyle   Harper

> Laura is fifteen and, in warm weather, working hard with Ma and Pa on their Dakota Territory claim. She earns what she can to help pay for Mary's courses at the College for the Blind, and, with her family, she spends the long, cold, but friend-filled winters in town.

1941 AWARD

Call It Courage   Armstrong Sperry   Illustrated by the author   Macmillan

Mocked by the other boys because of his fear of the sea, Mafatu secretly takes a small boat and leaves his village. Alone on a terrifying ocean voyage, the boy, son of a Polynesian chief, overcomes his fear of the sea.

HONORS

Young Mac of Fort Vancouver   Mary Jane Carr
Illustrated by Richard Holberg   Crowell

> Traveling west to Fort Vancouver in 1832, Young Mac is determined to become a fur-trading Northman and not a full-fledged member of the white world. Contact with Dr. McLoughlan, head of the fort, and other white and mixed-heritage men causes him to reconsider his decision.

Blue Willow   Doris Gates   Illustrated by Paul Lantz   Viking

With her small family wandering from place to place so that Dad can find work, Janey has never really had a home or school or friends. Maybe the San Joaquin Valley will be the place where everything changes, a place where they can stay and she can finally bring the blue willow plate out for good.

Nansen   Anna Gertrude Hall   Illustrated by Boris Artzybasheff   Viking

Determined to learn as much as he can as a little boy (and even more determined as an adult), Fridtjof Nansen grows to be one of Norway's most famous citizens. He is an explorer who travels all the way to the North Pole, a statesman, and, most difficult of all, a fighter for world peace and a winner of the Nobel Peace Prize.

The Long Winter   Laura Ingalls Wilder   Illustrated by Helen Sewell
and Mildred Boyle   Harper

The Ingalls family, pioneering in the Dakota Territory, stoically endure a dreary succession of blizzards. Huddled in the family store, they and their neighbors must depend upon their ingenuity to prevent freezing and starvation.

1940 AWARD

Daniel Boone   James Daugherty   Illustrated by the author   Viking

A rugged frontiersman and a leader of pioneers, Daniel Boone starts life in Pennsylvania and ends it eighty-six years later in Missouri, an almost legendary character. Boone's longing for adventure, his bravery, and his foolishness are examined honestly in this biography that sings the praises of pioneer men and women in words and vigorous drawings.

HONORS

Boy with a Pack   Stephen W. Meader
Illustrated by Edward Shenton   Harcourt

Bill fills a backpack with things to sell in Ohio and, with two years of savings, leaves his New Hampshire mill town on foot. The 1837 journey is long and hard but filled with all kinds of adventures, danger, and amazing good luck.

Runner of the Mountain Tops: The Life of Louis Agassiz   Mabel Robinson
Illustrated by Lynd Ward   Random House

A brilliant naturalist and the founder of Harvard's Agassiz Museum, Louis Agassiz is realistically portrayed from his childhood in Switzerland through his years as a Harvard professor. Agassiz's fascination with all of nature and his great teaching ability are evident throughout the book.

The Singing Tree   Kate Seredy   Illustrated by the author   Viking

> Four years after the end of *The Good Master,* the First World War has started, and Mother, Jancsi, and cousin Kate are left to take care of the farm as Father and Uncle Sandor are called to fight. The three of them hold the farm together and make it a refuge for orphans, relatives, and even prisoners of war.

By the Shores of Silver Lake   Laura Ingalls Wilder
Illustrated by Helen Sewell and Mildred Boyle   Harper

> The Ingalls have not had a good crop since the grasshoppers came. Pa decides they will make one more move, this time to Dakota Territory. The family spends a happy winter taking in other settlers and earning money to send Mary, blind from scarlet fever, to a special school.

1939 AWARD

Thimble Summer   Elizabeth Enright   Illustrated by the author
Farrar & Rinehart

All kinds of good things seem to happen after Garnet finds the silver thimble in the dried-up river bed. The nine-year-old farm girl notices that the drought finally breaks, she has an exciting time being locked in the public library with a friend, and her pet pig wins a blue ribbon at the fair.

HONORS

Nino   Valenti Angelo   Illustrated by the author   Viking

> While his father works in America to earn their fare to California, Nino and his mother stay with his grandfather in his small Italian village. The little boy and his family and friends share holidays, trips to the city, and small but exciting adventures that create a memorable picture of turn-of-the-century Italy.

Mr. Popper's Penguins   Richard and Florence Atwater
Illustrated by Robert Lawson   Little, Brown

> From the moment he is given a penguin as a pet, Mr. Popper's life starts changing. He converts his basement into an ice rink, finds a friend for his lonely bird, and suddenly has twelve penguins to feed instead of one.

"Hello the Boat!"   Phyllis Crawford   Illustrated by Edward Laning   Holt

> The entire Doak family pitches in to get their store-boat from Pittsburgh to Cincinnati in 1817. Along the Ohio River, settlers shout out, "Hello the boat!" and the family eagerly pushes the boat ashore and enthusiastically opens the store. On their way, the Doaks encounter thieves, learn about the history of the river area, and have a surprisingly good time.

Leader by Destiny: George Washington, Man and Patriot   Jeanette Eaton
Illustrated by Jack Manley Rose   Harcourt

> Not a man who plans what he wants but rather one who allows things to shape him and his future, George Washington lives a life full of adventure and responsibility as he grows up. The fifty-two years of his life that Eaton covers contain much of the history and many of the famous people of his time.

Penn   Elizabeth Janet Gray   Illustrated by George Gillett Whitney   Viking

> Until he converts to the Quaker religion, William Penn leads a privileged upper-class life. Then he loses everything and is imprisoned. After fighting hard for religious freedom, Penn is allowed to go to America and found the new colony of Pennsylvania, based on the principles for which he fought.

1938 AWARD

The White Stag   Kate Seredy   Illustrated by the author   Viking

Based on legends about the founding of Hungary, this stirring story begins with Nimrod receiving a prophesy from God. He tells his people to follow the White Stag and Nimrod's sons to the west. During their long and dangerous journey, the people move valiantly westward until the birth of Attila, who one day leads them heroically into what becomes Hungary.

HONORS

Pecos Bill   James Cloyd Bowman
Illustrated by Laura Bannon   Little, Brown

> Raised by coyotes and able to speak to animals, Pecos Bill reluctantly accepts the knowledge that he is one of those dreaded inhuman humans. He becomes a cowboy and does things in legendary proportion: busting up a cyclone, breaking up a cattle rustling gang, and rounding up 39,000,000 cattle and driving them to market.

Bright Island   Mabel Robinson   Illustrated by Lynd Ward   Random House

> Strong, independent, and committed to life on her family's small island off the coast of Maine, Thankful very reluctantly agrees to attend school on the mainland. There, life is so foreign that she initially feels like a total outsider among the other high school students.

On the Banks of Plum Creek   Laura Ingalls Wilder
Illustrated by Helen Sewell and Mildred Boyle   Harper

> After finally reaching Minnesota and planting a wheat crop, the Ingalls lose it to a horde of grasshoppers. Determined to stay, Pa goes to work for other farmers.

Laura goes to school, shares adventures with friends, but most of all enjoys the moments when her family is together and Pa is back playing the fiddle.

1937 AWARD

Roller Skates   Ruth Sawyer   Illustrated by Valenti Angelo   Viking

Her wealthy parents in Europe, Lucinda spends a glorious year living with two teachers, skating all over New York City, and making friends everywhere. The people she meets, whether it is her impoverished musician neighbor or the hansom cab driver, appreciate her energy, friendliness, and determination.

HONORS

The Golden Basket   Ludwig Bemelmans   Illustrated by the author   Viking

A staid English father and his two little daughters visit Bruges, Belgium, and stay at the Golden Basket Hotel. The girls and the hotel owner's son enjoy exploring the famous city. While visiting a cathedral, they meet twelve little girls standing in two straight lines, the youngest and spunkiest being Madeline.

Winterbound   Margery Bianco   Illustrated by Kate Seredy   Viking

With both of their parents gone for months, nineteen-year-old Kay and sixteen-year-old Garry take on managing both the rented cottage and their younger brother and sister. During a long, cold, but very exciting Depression-era winter, they make friends, earn and save money, and gain strength and independence.

The Codfish Musket   Agnes Hewes
Illustrated by Armstrong Sperry   Doubleday

Even as a youngster, Dan has a keen eye for fine rifles and arms. On a mission to Washington for his Boston employer, Dan becomes secretary to Thomas Jefferson. The president sends him into the frontier with a message for Merriwether Lewis, but along the way Dan spots gun thieves arming the Indians. He defeats them and delivers his message, finally returning to Washington.

Whistler's Van   Idwal Jones   Illustrated by Zhenya Gay   Viking

After his grandfather disappears one night with a cart and pony, Gwilyn decides he wants a chance to wander through Wales as well. When the Ringos, a family of gypsies, appear at the farmhouse and whistle, Gwilyn goes off with them for a summer full of music, adventure, and, most important, horses.

Phebe Fairchild: Her Book   Lois Lenski   Illustrated by the author   Stokes

When Phebe's mother decides to join Phebe's father on a sea voyage, the ten-year-old is sent to stay with relatives in the country. Life in 1830 rural Connecticut at first seems rigid to Phebe, and her copy of *Mother Goose* is a constant source of support. The child comes to appreciate her relatives, their simple life, their generosity, and their sense of fun.

Audubon   Constance Rourke   Illustrated by James MacDonald with 12 colored plates from original Audubon prints   Harcourt Brace

Despite mysterious beginnings, John James Audubon manages to leave France and go to America. He marries but continues to traipse the countryside in search of birds and small animals to paint. Carefully researched, the book offers a well-rounded look at the man who became known for his nineteenth-century paintings of American birds.

1936 AWARD

Caddie Woodlawn   Carol Ryrie Brink
Illustrated by Kate Seredy   Macmillan

Eleven years old in 1864, Caddie roams the woods and rivers of western Wisconsin with her brothers as her mother relentlessly tries to make her into a young "lady." The mischievous redhead's adventures with Indians and pioneers are full of fun and excitement.

HONORS

Young Walter Scott   Elizabeth Janet Gray   Illustrated by Kate Seredy   Viking

Despite years of living with country relatives, Walter is determined not to let his lame leg stand in his way once he is at home again. This lively, fictionalized biography transports readers to late eighteenth-century Edinburgh, Scotland, and offers an engrossing introduction to the life of the famous novelist.

The Good Master   Kate Seredy   Illustrated by the author   Viking

Jancsi is fascinated by his city cousin Kate's daring and reckless behavior. Whether she is stopping a stampede of horses, nearly drowning in the river, or running off with gypsies, she is a marvel and a delight to the Hungarian country folk.

All Sail Set: A Romance of the Flying Cloud   Armstrong Sperry   Winston

Fifteen-year-old Thach goes to work for the great Donald McKay making drawings of his plans for the clipper ship *Flying Cloud*. The ship completed, Thach becomes an apprentice, sails around the Horn, is initiated by "Neptune," contends with mutineers, and nearly loses his life in a shipboard fire.

Honk, the Moose   Phil Stong   Illustrated by Kurt Wiese   Dodd, Mead

The temperature is thirty below zero and the snow is seven feet deep when the boys find a moose in Ivar's father's stable. The town is in an uproar as everyone tries to think of ways to get the gentle and very funny beast to leave.

1935 AWARD

Dobry   Monica Shannon   Illustrated by Atanas Katchamakoff   Viking

Bulgarian peasant boy Dobry tries to convince his mother that he must be an artist. He does not want to plow the fields as his ancestors did. Dobry's grandfather understands, but until Dobry sculpts a beautiful nativity scene in the snow to prove his talents, his mother is not convinced.

HONORS

Davy Crockett   Constance Rourke   Illustrated by James MacDonald   Harcourt

Davy Crockett is a bigger-than-life character: he is a pioneer, hunter, teller of tales, soldier, statesman, and legendary American hero. Rourke writes a well-researched and well-documented biography filled with anecdotes and comments by Crockett and his contemporaries.

Pageant of Chinese History   Elizabeth Seeger
Illustrated by Bernard Watkins   Longmans, Green

Using a conversational style, Seeger leads the reader through Chinese history starting with mythical and legendary times. Then she writes about each of the dynasties, ending with the Manchu in 1912 and the beginning of the republic. Political and cultural history are the focus of most of the book.

A Day on Skates: The Story of a Dutch Picnic   Hilda Van Stockum
Illustrated by the author   Harper

The canals of Holland are finally frozen solid, and the headmaster has a surprise. He takes the children on an all-day skating picnic. In spite of a few accidents, it is a thoroughly enjoyable time. Many black-and-white drawings and eight full-color illustrations show the festive atmosphere of the day.

1934 AWARD

Invincible Louisa: The Story of the Author of Little Women
Cornelia Meigs   Little, Brown

The life of Louisa May Alcott is chronicled through her lively involvement with family and friends. Incidents reveal that her invincible spirit keeps the family afloat during the darkest of times and always keeps them happy. Family photographs and a chronology are included.

HONORS

The Winged Girl of Knossos   Erick Berry, pseud. (Allena Best)
Illustrated by the author   Appleton

Spirited, athletic, and beautiful Inas, daughter of Daidalos, helps her father with his flying experiments on the Isle of Crete during the time of King Minos. Having to leave Crete hurriedly, she does so by flying out on a glider built by her father.

The Big Tree of Bunlahy: Stories of My Own Countryside   Padraic Colum
Illustrated by Jack Yeats   Macmillan

Twelve fine old Irish tales and one original one are woven together by the storyteller who introduces each story. All are said to have been heard under the Tree of Bunlahy, the great elm tree with big, smooth stones under it. There the villagers would sit and listen to these tales of animals, heroes, and leprechans.

The ABC Bunny   Wanda Gág   Illustrated by the author;
hand lettered by Howard Gág   Coward

Lithographs filled with curved lines show a bunny romping through his day. After being scared out of his bed by a crashing apple, the bunny meets many animals. Each large, bright red letter of the alphabet is accompanied by a text that carries the ABC lesson along in a rhythmic manner. The song, with words and music, is included.

Glory of the Seas   Agnes Hewes   Illustrated by N. C. Wyeth   Knopf

The exciting early days of the clipper ships, the controversial Fugitive Slave Law, and the inner conflict caused by civil disobedience are at the center of this story set in Boston in the 1850s. When the *Flying Cloud* sails to San Francisco in just eighty-nine days, many Bostonians dream of sailing to California.

The Apprentice of Florence   Anne Kyle
Illustrated by Erick Berry, pseud. (Allena Best)   Houghton

Nemo, a sixteen-year-old Florentine apprentice, is sent to Constantinople on business in 1453. The city is besieged by Turks, and Nemo is hurt. On his return, young Christopher Columbus tells him that his father, thought to be dead, is alive. More adventures ensue as Nemo searches for his lost father.

New Land   Sarah Schmidt   Illustrated by Frank Dobias   McBride

It is the 1930s when Dad, the seventeen-year-old twins, and their younger sister arrive in Wyoming to homestead on an unproved claim. Rivalries on the football field and in the new vocational school, a blinding snowstorm, and troubles with the "big man" are overcome, and a new home is established.

Swords of Steel   Elsie Singmaster   Illustrated by David Hendrickson   Houghton

Although he has heard talk of the differences between the North and the South, it is not until 1859, when his beloved, free black friend is kidnapped to be sold, that John feels personal involvement in the conflict. In six years John grows from childhood to manhood with the Civil War intruding on and then enveloping his life.

The Forgotten Daughter   Caroline Dale Snedeker
Illustrated by Dorothy P. Lathrop   Doubleday

When his wife dies in childbirth while he is traveling, the Roman centurion is told that both mother and child are dead. His daughter is subjected to the hardships of second-century life as a slave. Eventually she falls in love with a high-born Roman, and the plague unites her with her father.

1933 AWARD

Young Fu of the Upper Yangtze   Elizabeth Foreman Lewis
Illustrated by Kurt Wiese   Winston

The empress has died and political life is in turmoil when Young Fu and his mother move from their village to Chungking so that he can be apprenticed to a coppersmith. Young Fu must constantly use his wits to protect his mother and himself from thieves and rascals.

HONORS

Children of the Soil: A Story of Scandinavia   Nora Burglon
Illustrated by Edgar Parin d'Aulaire   Doubleday

Two very poor but ambitious and industrious children live with their mother in Sweden at the turn of the twentieth century. The soil they hoe is poor, their crab trap washes out to sea, and a weaving contest is lost to the gentry. With a little help from a Tomte and a lot of work on their part, they acquire some livestock and the promise of a happier future.

Swift Rivers   Cornelia Meigs
Illustrated by Forrest W. Orr   Little, Brown

When his mean-spirited uncle locks him out of the house where he was raised, Chris knows it is time to become a man. The harsh 1835 Wisconsin winter and the bountiful woods lead him to try floating logs down to St. Louis. As a part of the early days of the logging industry, Chris has many adventures on the river.

The Railroad to Freedom: A Story of the Civil War   Hildegarde Swift
Illustrated by James Daugherty   Harcourt

> Harriet Tubman, a slave, escapes from the South but goes back again and again, leading three hundred other slaves North to freedom via the dangerous Underground Railroad. The horrifying yet often thrilling adventures are based on incidents from Tubman's life.

1932 AWARD

Waterless Mountain   Laura Adams Armer
Illustrated by Sidney and Laura Adams Armer   Longmans, Green

Destined to become a medicine man, introspective Younger Brother learns the songs and stories of the Navajo Indians and begins to create songs of his own. Skillfully interwoven into the story are the early twentieth-century culture and heritage of the tribe.

HONORS

Jane's Island   Marjorie Allee
Illustrated by Maitland de Gorgoza   Houghton

> Ellen, a college freshman, spends the summer with twelve-year-old Jane in Woods Hole, Massachusetts, where Jane's father is a marine biologist. The girls enjoy light summer adventures while fishing and picnicking. Jane is a competent naturalist who imparts a good measure of scientific information throughout the story.

Truce of the Wolf and Other Tales of Old Italy   Mary Gould Davis
Illustrated by Jay Van Everen   Harcourt

> Seven widely varied Italian stories tell of such things as Saint Francis taming a menacing wolf, of an obstinate and heroic donkey, and of how a street in Florence was named. The tales, all told with a bit of Italian folk humor, come from many sources, including a Tuscan peasant woman and *The Decameron*.

Calico Bush   Rachel Field   Illustrated by Allen Lewis   Macmillan

> In 1743, twelve-year-old Marguerite is bound out to a family in Maine. Discriminated against by the parents because she is French, she finds happiness with the children as they all face hardships and the rigors of life in the Maine wilderness.

The Fairy Circus   Dorothy P. Lathrop   Illustrated by the author Macmillan

> When the circus tent goes up, it is so big that it encloses the places where the fairies live. They all scramble for the best view, and when it is over they decide to have a circus of their own. The fairies and woodland animals use grand imaginations as they re-create the circus in their own way.

Out of the Flame   Eloise Lownsbery
Illustrated by Elizabeth Tyler Wolcott   Longmans, Green

> In the sixteenth century, Pierre is first a page then a squire as he becomes trained
> to be a knight in the court of Francis I. He attends tournaments, visits with great
> intellectuals, and learns music and botany with the royal children. Before the story
> ends, he and the children are abducted and released by pirates.

Boy of the South Seas   Eunice Tietjens
Illustrated by Myrtle Sheldon   Coward

> When a ship arrives in the harbor of the Marquesas Islands, young Teiki's curios-
> ity gets ahold of him, and he climbs aboard and falls asleep. He awakens when the
> vessel is under sail and there is no turning back. At the island of Moorea, he swims
> ashore and makes a new life for himself.

1931 AWARD

The Cat Who Went to Heaven   Elizabeth Coatsworth
Illustrated by Lynd Ward   Macmillan

A starving Japanese artist is commissioned to paint the death of Buddha. He longs to
include his gentle cat, Good Fortune, among the animals, but legend says cats cannot
enter heaven. Because of her goodness, he paints her, and the little animal dies of happiness. When the priest objects, the painting miraculously changes to show Buddha
accepting the cat.

HONORS

Mountains Are Free   Julia Davis Adams
Illustrated by Theodore Nadejen   Dutton

> Bruno, a young Swiss orphan who is being raised by the Tells, suddenly decides
> to become a page to an Austrian, saying he will return when he can earn his own
> way. The stirring of democracy causes conflicts as the Swiss try to rebel against the
> harshness of their Habsburg rulers.

Garram the Hunter: A Boy of the Hill Tribes   Herbert Best
Illustrated by Erick Berry, pseud. (Allena Best)   Doubleday

> Hoping to find an ally for his chieftain father, Garram is sent to stay with the emir
> and becomes a favorite of the ruler. When he returns home, he discovers not only a
> plot to imprison his father but receives word that the eastern tribes are threatening.

Meggy MacIntosh   Elizabeth Janet Gray
Illustrated by Marguerite de Angeli   Doubleday

> In 1775 orphaned fifteen-year-old Meggy leaves her native Scotland to sail for the
> colony of North Carolina. There she joins Flora MacDonald, who had helped Bon-

nie Prince Charlie escape. Meggy becomes involved in the revolutionary cause and moves away from Flora, a loyalist.

Spice and the Devil's Cave   Agnes Hewes   Illustrated by Lynd Ward   Knopf

At a workshop in Portugal, Bartholomew Diaz, Vasco da Gama, and Ferdinand Magellan gather to discuss their theory that an all-sea route around the Cape of Good Hope, also known as the Devil's Cave, must exist. The theft by pirates of the only known maps adds interest and intrigue.

Queer Person   Ralph Hubbard   Illustrated by Harold von Schmidt   Doubleday

He can neither hear nor talk, and at age four he wanders into a camp of Pikuni Indians. His silence earns him the name Queer Person, and he is raised by an old woman in the tribe. During his test of bravery, he rescues the chief's lost son from the Crows, and it is revealed that they are brothers.

Ood-Le-Uk the Wanderer   Alice Lide and Margaret Johansen
Illustrated by Raymond Lufkin   Little, Brown

An Alaskan Eskimo caught on an ice floe crosses the Bering Straight. After years of wandering, he returns home to establish trade between his tribe and the Siberian tribesmen. Once known as a weakling, after his hazardous adventures he is known to be a brave man.

The Dark Star of Itzá: The Story of a Pagan Princess   Alida Malkus
Illustrated by Lowell Houser   Harcourt

When the khan of Chichén Itzá kidnaps the betrothed of another Mayan chieftain, war breaks out, and the city falls into the hands of the Toltecs. The seventeen-year-old daughter of Chichén Itzá's chief priest agrees to be the sacrifice that will save her city, but her father bravely finds a way to save her.

Floating Island   Anne Parrish   Illustrated by the author   Harper

All packed up and on board a ship bound for the tropics, a doll family and their doll house land on Floating Island after their ship wrecks. They adapt well to the island but soon realize that dolls can never be happy if they are away from children for too long. They then arrange their own rescue.

1930 AWARD

Hitty, Her First Hundred Years   Rachel Field
Illustrated by Dorothy P. Lathrop   Macmillan

Carved from a block of mountain ash a hundred years before, the six-and-a-half-inch doll now sits secure in the antique shop window and writes her memoirs. She recounts the adventures she had with many different people in places around the world. Illustrations show Hitty in many styles of clothing in her life thus far.

HONORS

Vaino   Julia Davis Adams   Illustrated by Lempi Ostman   Dutton

Ancient legends of Finland, the lives of three children, and the Finnish Revolution of 1917 are blended together to tell a story filled with strong patriotic spirit. Vaino and his older brother and sister become a part of the revolution that finally frees Finland of foreign domination.

A Daughter of the Seine: The Life of Madame Roland   Jeanette Eaton   Harper

Madame Roland's life coincides with the French Revolution. The historical biography describes the childhood, married life, and tragic execution by guillotine of this remarkable woman. Madame Roland is intelligent and strongly supports the revolution, and her salon is depicted as the headquarters of much political activity.

The Jumping-Off Place   Marian Hurd McNeely
Illustrated by William Siegel   Longmans, Green

When the uncle who cared for them dies, four children pull up stakes in Wisconsin and move to South Dakota. There they weather adventures, hardships, and squatters for the fourteen months it takes to make homesteaders owners of the land.

Pran of Albania   Elizabeth Miller
Illustrated by Maud and Miska Petersham   Doubleday

In post-World War I Albania amidst a threat of attack from Slavs, fourteen-year-old Pran falls in love. Rather than submit to an arranged marriage, she vows to never marry. After a truce is made, Pran realizes the man she loves is the same man her parents had arranged for her to marry.

Little Blacknose   Hildegarde Swift   Illustrated by Lynd Ward   Harcourt

Little Blacknose is none other than the DeWitt Clinton Engine, the first locomotive built for the New York Central Railway. The personified engine tells of his life until he becomes enthroned in New York's Grand Central Terminal.

The Tangle-Coated Horse and Other Tales   Ella Young
Illustrated by Vera Bock   Longmans, Green

The Fionn Saga, the stories of Finn McCool known in every Gaelic-speaking part of Scotland and all over Ireland, is retold with vigor. The stories begin when McCool is a small boy learning about his heritage and his crafts and end three hundred years later when his son returns from the country of the Ever-Young.

1929 AWARD

The Trumpeter of Krakow: A Tale of the Fifteenth Century   Eric P. Kelly
Illustrated by Angela Pruszynska   Macmillan

For two hundred years the Charnetski family has guarded Poland's most famous jewel. When the czar of Russia finds out about the valuable crystal, he sends men to steal it before the Charnetskis can get it to the king of Poland. Adventure, mystery, and self-sacrifice fill this medieval story set in Krakow.

HONORS

The Pigtail of Ah Lee Ben Loo   John Bennett
Illustrated by the author   Longmans, Green

> Many original stories in prose and verse, and one brief wordless story, are illustrated with two hundred intriguing and often funny silhouettes. The stories are filled with robust and irreverent humor: King Arthur's Sir Launcelot is called "Sir Launcelot de Id-i-otte"! Most of the stories first appeared in *St. Nicholas Magazine.*

Millions of Cats   Wanda Gág   Illustrated by the author   Coward

> A lonely old couple decides to get a cat. Searching for the prettiest one out of a whole hillside filled with cats, the man comes home with "hundreds of cats, thousands of cats, millions and billions and trillions of cats." When the cats fight about who is prettiest, only one is left.

The Boy Who Was   Grace Hallock
Illustrated by Harrie Wood   Dutton

> In 1927 Nino the goatherd shows an artist the wooden figures he has carved of famous Mediterranean people and proceeds to tell their stories, covering more than 3,000 years of history. He begins with tales of Odysseus, Pompeii, and the Crusades and then goes through the nineteenth century, occasionally including himself in the stories.

Clearing Weather   Cornelia Meigs   Illustrated by Frank Dobias   Little, Brown

> It is just after the American Revolution and the economy has not recovered. When young Nicholas Drury takes over his family's shipbuilding business, he struggles hard until the family fortune reverses itself with the successful design, construction, and voyage of the Jocasta, a forerunner of the clipper ship.

The Runaway Papoose   Grace Moon   Illustrated by Carl Moon   Doubleday

> Little Nah-tee runs away when outlaw Indians attack her family's camp. Her parents cannot find her and move on with the others. Nah-tee and a young

shepherd boy she meets have many adventures as they cross the mesa in search of her parents.

Tod of the Fens   Elinor Whitney   Illustrated by Warwick Goble   Macmillan

Fifteenth-century Boston, England, is the setting for the amusing tale of Tod, who lives with a band of men just outside of town. Prince Hal, later to become Henry V, roves about the town in various disguises. Tod, realizing what is happening, tells no one and plays along with the game that is afoot.

1928 AWARD

Gay-Neck, the Story of a Pigeon   Dhan Gopal Mukerji
Illustrated by Boris Artzybasheff   Dutton

Born in Calcutta, Gay-Neck has thrilling adventures, first traveling all over India and later working as a carrier pigeon for the Indian Army in France during World War I. Eventually he returns to his young owner in India. Sometimes the story is told by Mukerji and at other times by Gay-Neck the pigeon.

HONORS

Downright Dencey   Caroline Dale Snedeker
Illustrated by Maginel Wright Barney   Doubleday

A Nantucket Quaker community during the War of 1812 provides the background for the story of a young girl named Dencey who first becomes involved with outcast Sammie when she hurls a stone at him. Ashamed, she tries to make amends but Sammie's trust must be won, and that is not easy for Dencey.

The Wonder Smith and His Son: A Tale from the Golden Childhood of the World
Retold by Ella Young   Illustrated by Boris Artzybasheff   Longmans, Green

Fourteen stories of Gubbaun Saor, a mythological creature of Ireland, have been retold from tales the author heard from English and Gaelic storytellers. The stories capture the lilting cadence of the Irish language and are enhanced by the graphics.

1927 AWARD

Smoky, the Cowhorse   Will James   Illustrated by the author   Scribner

Born free on the open range, Smoky roams the hills until he is caught and gentled by Clint, a cowboy. Stolen and cruelly treated, Smoky kills his captor and runs as an outlaw. Captured again, he becomes a rodeo horse until once more he meets up with Clint and lives out his life on the range where he was born.

HONOR

No record.

1926 AWARD

Shen of the Sea: A Book for Children   Arthur Bowie Chrisman
Illustrated by Else Hasselriis   Dutton

Sixteen charming and funny original stories are told in traditional folktale style. Most of the stories explain the origins of things like printing, chopsticks, and gunpowder. In several stories, the main character, always reacting the opposite of what is expected, is tricked by the smarter, minor characters.

HONOR

The Voyagers: Being Legends and Romances of Atlantic Discovery
Padraic Colum   Illustrated by Wildred Jones   Macmillan

> Convinced that there is another land far away, Portugal's Prince Henry the Navigator gathers together all those who might know anything about it. In a high tower that overlooks the Atlantic Ocean, stories of legends and voyages are told along with those of the discoveries of Columbus and Ponce de León.

1925 AWARD

Tales from Silver Lands   Charles Finger
Illustrated by Paul Honoré   Doubleday

Nineteen stories that Finger gathered from South American Indian villagers are retold retaining their original flavor. Included are captivating tales of witches, giants, and strange enchantments.

HONORS

Nicholas: A Manhattan Christmas Story   Anne Carroll Moore
Illustrated by Jay Van Everen   Putnam

> Nicholas, eight inches high, is a little boy from Holland who visits New York City for a few months in the 1920s. While there, he attends parties, visits famous landmarks, and learns about the Dutch influence on the city. His first party is at the library, where he is introduced to many book characters.

The Dream Coach   Anne Parrish and Dillwyn Parish
Illustrated by the authors   Macmillan

> The Dream Coach is pulled by one hundred misty horses. Helped by little angels, it travels the night sky dispensing dreams. Four children are introduced in turn, and their fairy-tale-like dreams, often involving inanimate objects that come to life, are shared.

1924 AWARD

The Dark Frigate   Charles Hawes
Illustrated by A. L. Ripley   Little, Brown

A seagoing adventure turns sour when the *Rose of Devon* is seized in mid-ocean by pirates. The vile, ruthless men force nineteen-year-old Philip to be a part of the pirate crew, and the hangman awaits his return to England. Set in the time of King Charles, the story does not romanticize piracy.

HONOR

> No record.

1923 AWARD

The Voyages of Doctor Dolittle   Hugh Lofting
Illustrated by the author   Stokes

Fun and nonsense reign as Dr. John Dolittle, a medical doctor and naturalist who has the ability to talk to animals, sets sail for Spider Monkey Island. There he unites two tribes, becomes king, and sails home inside the 70,000-year-old great glass sea snail. The story is told by the doctor's nine-and-a-half-year-old assistant.

HONOR

> No record.

1922 AWARD

The Story of Mankind   Hendrik Willem van Loon
Illustrated by the author   Boni & Liveright

Speaking directly to the reader, the author provides a fascinating picture of history from cave peoples to the present (1920). Ideas, movements, and people are more important than dates, and history is shown as something that builds upon itself.

HONORS

*The Old Tobacco Shop: A True Account of What Befell
a Little Boy in Search of Adventure*   William Bowen
Illustrated by Reginald Birch   Macmillan

> Fred is befriended by the hunchback who runs the tobacco shop. Warned never
> to smoke the magic tobacco in the porcelain jar shaped like a "Chinaman's head,"
> Fred stays away from it for a long time. One day he falters and suddenly finds him-
> self involved in high adventure on the Spanish Main.

The Golden Fleece and the Heroes Who Lived before Achilles   Padraic Colum
Illustrated by Willy Pogany   Macmillan

> The ancient triumphs and tragedies of the Greek myths are woven through the
> central story of Jason and his quest for the Golden Fleece. The many stories told
> by Orpheus to the sailors in the story might be the very ones that the Argonauts
> heard on their long voyage.

The Great Quest   Charles Hawes Illustrated by George Varian   Little, Brown

> Twelve-year-old Josiah tells of how his Uncle Seth is tricked by an old friend into
> selling his shop and buying a ship. Thinking they are going in search of gold, Josiah
> and his uncle find themselves unwillingly involved in the slave trade and at odds
> with the crew.

Cedric the Forester   Bernard Marshall   Illustrated by J. Scott Williams   Appleton

> Cedric, son of a thirteenth-century forester, saves Sir Richard's son and is made
> his squire. Taught to read and fight, Cedric becomes the best crossbowman in
> England, and, at the Battle of the Eagles, he is knighted.

The Windy Hill   Cornelia Meigs
Illustrated by Elmer and Berta Hader   Macmillan

> A brother and sister visit their older cousin in New England. Their cousin was once
> jovial but is now mysteriously irritable and preoccupied. A chance meeting with
> the beeman leads to their hearing stories about their own family's history. As they
> listen, the two children start to understand the cause of their cousin's anxiety.

The Caldecott Awards

2007–1938

2007 CALDECOTT AWARD

FLOTSAM
David Wiesner
Clarion

DAVID WIESNER

Flotsam is a cinematic unfolding of discovery. A vintage camera washed up on the beach provides a young boy with a surprising view of fantastical images from the bottom of the sea. From fish eye to lens eye, readers see a frame-by-frame narrative of lush marinescapes ebbing and flowing from the real to the surreal.

"Telling tales through imagery is what storytellers have done through the ages. Wiesner's wordless tale resonates with visual images that tell his story with clever wit and lively humor," said Caldecott Medal Committee Chair Janice Del Negro.

2007 HONOR BOOKS

Gone Wild: An Endangered Animal Alphabet
David McLimans   Walker

This black-and-white iconic alphabet is sophisticated enough to intrigue and capti-vate readers of any age. A contemporary interpretation of an illuminated alphabet melds animals and letters into twenty-six unique and elegant graphic images.

Moses: When Harriet Tubman Led Her People to Freedom
Carole Boston Weatherford   Illustrated by Kadir Nelson
Hyperion/Jump at the Sun

Nelson's dramatic renderings evoke the spiritual and physical journey of Harriet Tub-man. Emotionally powerful images combined with poetically evocative text portray a strong woman who followed her star to an extraordinary destiny.

2006 AWARD

The Hello, Goodbye Window   Norton Juster   Illustrated by Chris Raschka
Michael di Capua Books

In this sunny portrait of familial love, a little girl tells us about her everyday experiences visiting her grandparents' house. Raschka's style resembles the spontaneous drawings of children, perfectly mirroring the guileless young narrator's exuberant voice. White space balances the density of the layered colors, creating a visual experience that is surprisingly sophisticated.

HONORS

Rosa   Nikki Giovanni   Illustrated by Bryan Collier   Henry Holt

From the arresting cover through the endpapers, *Rosa*, with Giovanni's spare, elegant prose and Collier's iconic illustrations, celebrates the quiet courage of Rosa Parks. Radiant watercolors of faces and hands highlighted against the edges of richly colored collages create a distinguished work of art.

Zen Shorts   Jon J. Muth   Illustrated by the author   Scholastic

Muth's story of inquisitive siblings befriending a wise panda is told through luminous watercolors interwoven with three lessons, set apart by starkly contrasting, Asian-inspired brush paintings. The interplay of artistic styles elegantly conveys the gentle, timeless messages of self-knowledge and acceptance.

Hot Air: The (Mostly) True Story of the First Hot-Air Balloon Ride
Marjorie Priceman   Illustrated by the author   Anne Schwartz/Atheneum

Energetic lines and rich watercolors animate this aerial adventure over eighteenth-century France. Priceman, who received a 1996 Caldecott honor for *Zin! Zin! Zin! A Violin*, combines spare text, dynamic design, and masterful perspective to illuminate the humor and high jinks of three animals swept up in the winds of history.

Song of the Water Boatman and Other Pond Poems
Joyce Sidman   Illustrated by Beckie Prange   Houghton

Eleven joyful songs of everyday pond life throughout the seasons are celebrated through this elegant and satisfying combination of visual drama, poetry, and scientific facts. The organic lines of Prange's exceptionally executed, hand-colored woodblock illustrations enlarge upon Sidman's expressive nature-themed poems.

2005 AWARD

Kitten's First Full Moon   Kevin Henkes   Illustrated by the author
Greenwillow

Henkes employs boldly outlined organic shapes and shades of black, white, and gray with rose undertones on creamy paper to tell a simple story of a kitten who mistakes the moon for a bowl of milk. The moon, the flowers, the fireflies' lights, and the kitten's eyes create a comforting circle motif. The gouache and colored-pencil illustrations project a varied page design that rhythmically paces the spare text.

HONORS

The Red Book   Barbara Lehman   Illustrated by the author
Houghton

> With a simplicity that belies their depth, Lehman's nuanced watercolor illustrations transport a city girl, an island boy, and the viewer beyond their familiar worlds. This wordless picture book offers an enticing visual journey with surprising twists and reveals the mysterious power of books.

Coming On Home Soon   Jacqueline Woodson
Illustrated by E. B. Lewis   Putnam

> Evocative watercolor paintings illuminate a story of cross-generational love and convey the longing of a child anticipating her mother's return. Lewis's portraiture and attention to light sources, from cold winter hues to warm interior tones, reflect the loneliness of the child and the comforting strength of her grandmother.

Knuffle Bunny: A Cautionary Tale   Mo Willems   Illustrated by the author
Hyperion

> An ordinary trip to the laundromat with Dad becomes a hilarious epic drama of miscommunication when Trixie realizes that her beloved stuffed animal is left behind. This energetic comedy, illustrated with an unconventional combination of sepia-tone photographs and wry cartoon ink sketches, charms both parents and children.

2004 AWARD

The Man Who Walked between the Towers
Mordicai Gerstein   Illustrated by the author   Roaring Book Press

This true story recounts the daring feat of a spirited young Frenchman who walked a tightrope between the World Trade Center twin towers in 1974. His joy in dancing on a thin wire high above Manhattan and the awe of the spectators in the streets far below are captured in exquisite ink and oil paintings that perfectly complement the spare, lyrical text.

HONORS

Ella Sarah Gets Dressed   Margaret Chodos-Irvine
Illustrated by the author   Harcourt

> Standing in front of her wardrobe, Ella Sarah selects her attire and makes her own fashion statement. Cheerful, bold colors outlined in white emphasize Ella Sarah's freedom and confidence. Pink polka-dots on an orange background and blue-green rickrack on the borders of the jacket flap foreshadow her unique outfit.

What Do You Do with a Tail like This?   Steve Jenkins and Robin Page
Illustrated by the authors   Houghton

> This innovative guessing book delivers a fun and playful science lesson on thirty animals' body parts: ears, eyes, mouths, noses, feet, and tails. The artist uses exquisite cut-paper collage to detail basic forms combined with clever placement of the spare text to create an interactive visual display.

Don't Let the Pigeon Drive the Bus!   Mo Willems
Illustrated by the author   Hyperion

> A persistent pigeon asks, pleads, cajoles, wheedles, connives, negotiates, demands, and uses emotional blackmail in attempts to get behind the wheel. Pigeon will not take no for an answer and puts the reader on the spot, using an escalating series of tactics. Perfectly paced, every line and blank space in the deceptively simple illustrations are essential to this distinguished work.

2003 AWARD

My Friend Rabbit   Eric Rohmann   Illustrated by the author
Roaring Brook Press

Mouse shares his brand-new toy airplane with his friend Rabbit, and no one can predict the disastrous—but hilarious—results. When the airplane lands in a tree, the chaos only builds as Rabbit drags, pushes, and carries the whole neighborhood, including Elephant, Hippo, and Crocodile, to aid in the rescue. Eric Rohmann's hand-colored relief prints express a vibrant energy through solid black outlines, lightly textured backgrounds, and a robust use of color.

HONORS

The Spider and the Fly   Mary Howitt
Illustrated by Tony DiTerlizzi   Simon & Schuster

>DiTerlizzi's wickedly delicious tribute to silent film—based on the cautionary tale penned by Mary Howitt in 1829—presents an old-fashioned cackling villain and a naive damsel in distress in this ambient, moody picture book with all the allure of the flickering silver screen. Skillful use of tone, line, and perspective add to the mystery of this melodramatic tale, executed entirely in eerie shades of black and white.

Hondo & Fabian   Peter McCarty   Illustrated by the author   Henry Holt

>A beach outing for the dog and a full day at home for the cat are skillfully interwoven in this quiet tale of friendship. Spare text describes the day's events while soft, glowing illustrations tell the real story of parallel activities with subtle humor. McCarty's design choices from font and page layout to size and inviting cover art show great attention to detail in this masterfully executed picture book.

Noah's Ark   Jerry Pinkney   Illustrated by the author   SeaStar

>In this striking rendition of Noah and the Great Flood, Jerry Pinkney has integrated the well-known story from Genesis with masterful pencil and watercolor illustrations to create a stunning whole. Vibrant paintings evoke the tone of the story from lush, sweeping views of the earth to intricate details of the massive ark, myriad animals, Noah and his family, and finally to the restoration of the planet.

2002 AWARD

>*The Three Pigs*   David Wiesner   Illustrated by the author   Clarion

In *The Three Pigs*, the plot and form of a familiar folktale unravel as the pigs are huffed and puffed off the page and into a new world. The trio cavorts through scenes from a nursery rhyme to a fairy tale, liberating other characters on the fly. Using a range of artistic styles and thrilling perspectives, Wiesner plays with the structure and conventions of traditional storytelling, redefining the picture book.

HONORS

Martin's Big Words: The Life of Dr. Martin Luther King, Jr.
Doreen Rappaport   Illustrated by Bryan Collier
Jump at the Sun/Hyperion

>In this picture-book biography of Martin Luther King Jr., Rappaport's spare text and carefully chosen quotes are carried to a powerful emotional level by Collier's art. From the smiling, inviting image on the cover to each striking double spread

the artist portrays significant events evoking King's purpose, telling readers that "his big words are alive for us today."

The Dinosaurs of Waterhouse Hawkins: An Illuminating History of Mr. Waterhouse Hawkins, Artist and Lecturer   Barbara Kerley
Illustrated by Brian Selznick   Scholastic

With a sense of showmanship echoing the spectacle of Waterhouse Hawkins's own public presentations, this dramatic biography brings the work of the nineteenth-century dinosaur artist to life. Using a rich palette, theatrical staging, and monumental dimensions, Selznick creates an exquisite balance between illustration and design in this distinguished marriage of science and art.

The Stray Dog: From a True Story by Reike Sassa   Marc Simont
Illustrated by the author   HarperCollins

A chance encounter turns into a family love affair in this disarmingly simple, gently humorous, and emotionally satisfying tale. The soft palette and subtle touches in the distinctive watercolors perfectly capture the heroic actions of the young protagonists and convey the universal feelings of longing and belonging.

2001 AWARD

So You Want to Be President?   Judith St. George
Illustrated by David Small   Philomel

In illustrations rendered in a harmonious mix of watercolor, ink, and pastel chalk, Small employs wiry and expansive lines that echo political cartooning and invest this personable history of the presidency with imaginative detail, wry humor, and refreshing dignity. Small's illustrations capture the spirit of each president featured and provide a genuinely enlightening overview of this unique American institution.

HONORS

Casey at the Bat: A Ballad of the Republic Sung in the Year 1888
Ernest L. Thayer   Illustrated by Christopher Bing   Handprint

In the format of an 1888 scrapbook, the immortal ballad of Ernest Thayer finds new life in Christopher Bing's innovative treatment. Pen-and-ink scratchboard "engravings" in late nineteenth-century style seamlessly blend memorabilia and trompe l'oeil re-creations in an homage to the great American pastime.

Click, Clack, Moo: Cows That Type   Doreen Cronin
Illustrated by Betsy Lewin   Simon & Schuster

Farm-smart cows recycle a piece of outdated technology, a manual typewriter, to improve barnyard conditions. Lewin's illustrations help tell this tongue-in-cheek story about bovine agitators locking horns with Farmer Brown in a battle of will and wit that results in a comically satisfying conclusion.

Olivia   Ian Falconer   Illustrated by the author   Anne Schwartz/Atheneum

Olivia, an inquisitive, creative, confident young piglet, is "very good at wearing people out." With the touch of a minimalist, Falconer has created an exuberant character using deft black lines, delicate charcoal shading, generous white space, and spots of brilliant red.

2000 AWARD

Joseph Had a Little Overcoat   Simms Taback
Illustrated by the author   Viking

A resourceful and resilient tailor transforms his wornout overcoat into smaller and smaller garments. The book is illustrated in watercolor, gouache, pencil, ink, and collage. The patchwork layout of the pages, the two-dimensional paintings, and the exaggerated perspectives, reminiscent of the folk art tradition, are the very fabric that turn this overcoat into a story.

HONORS

A Child's Calendar: Poems   John Updike
Illustrated by Trina Schart Hyman   Holiday House

Twelve seasonal poems spanning the calendar year are accompanied by pen and ink and watercolor paintings that complement and enhance the text in this book of poetry. Hyman's affectionate illustrations expand Updike's poetic celebration of the changing of the seasons and holidays.

Sector 7   David Wiesner   Illustrated by the author   Clarion

A small boy on a class trip to the Empire State Building is transported by a friendly cloud to Sector 7, a great cloud factory high in the sky. Wiesner's striking and dramatic watercolors transform the childhood fantasy of figures in the clouds into an imaginative story without words.

When Sophie Gets Angry—Really, Really Angry . . .
Molly Bang   Illustrated by the author   Blue Sky/Scholastic

Sophie's indignation over being required to share a favorite toy with her sister leads her on a lonely internal journey from anger to equilibrium. Bang's use of color, line, and visual onomatopoeia combine with a deceptively simple text to create a visually stunning color of a child's journey through a temper tantrum and back to the warmth of her family.

The Ugly Duckling   Adapted and illustrated by Jerry Pinkney   Morrow

Panoramic end papers set the scene for the creation of the familiar Hans Christian Andersen tale, *The Ugly Duckling*. Each full-page spread is lush with color that befits the beauty of the naturalistic setting. Pinkney imbues the animals with personality without anthropomorphizing them.

1999 AWARD

Snowflake Bentley   Jacqueline Briggs Martin
Illustrated by Mary Azarian   Houghton

Mary Azarian's handsome woodcuts recall the impassioned life of a self-taught Vermont scientist, who as a boy was determined that one day his camera would capture the extraordinary and unique beauty of snowflakes.

HONORS

Duke Ellington: The Piano Prince and His Orchestra   Andrea Davis Pinkney
Illustrated by Brian Pinkney   Hyperion

Brian Pinkney masterfully uses color and movement to introduce today's children to the life and music of Duke Ellington, one of the great composers and jazz musicians of the twentieth century.

No, David!   David Shannon   Illustrated by the author   Blue Sky/Scholastic

David, a typically mischievous preschooler, is into everything he shouldn't be and "No, David!" is his mother's constant refrain. Shannon's childlike paintings and inventive use of line, color, and perspective bring David to life.

Snow   Uri Shulevitz   Illustrated by the author   Farrar Straus Giroux

This magical picture book captures in ink and watercolor washes the excitement of a small boy and his dog who, despite adult naysayers, steadfastly believe that snow is coming.

Tibet: Through the Red Box   Peter Sís   Illustrated by the author
Frances Foster/Farrar Straus Giroux

Through detailed art and lyrical text, Sís takes the reader on a literal, spiritual, and symbolic journey through time and memory to his childhood, his separation from a father far away in Tibet, and finally their reunion.

1998 AWARD

Rapunzel   Paul O. Zelinsky   Illustrated by the author   Dutton

Zelinsky retells the story based on the familiar Grimm's folktale as well as earlier French and Italian sources. The detailed oil paintings are inspired by Renaissance Masters' paintings.

HONORS

The Gardener   Sarah Stewart   Illustrated by David Small   Farrar Straus Giroux

Illustrations, combined with letters home, tell the story of Lydia Grace Finch, a young Depression-era heroine, who transforms her curmudgeonly uncle and his dreary urban neighborhood with her rooftop garden.

Harlem: A Poem   Walter Dean Myers
Illustrated by Christopher Myers   Scholastic

Christopher Myers uses ink, gouache, and cut-paper collage to interpret his father's ode to Harlem. A kaleidoscope of words and images leads the reader on a musical journey filled with sass and swing.

There Was an Old Lady Who Swallowed a Fly   Simms Taback
Illustrated by the author   Viking

The popular American folk song of the old woman with an insatiable taste for life is served up in a fresh presentation. The reader is treated to an insider's view of her progressively excessive appetite through expanding die-cut peepholes to the inevitable climax.

1997 AWARD

Golem   David Wisniewski   Illustrated by the author   Clarion

The Jews in sixteenth-century Prague turn to their rabbi during time of trouble. The Golem, created to protect the Jews, reflects the themes of power and redemption. How the rabbi deals with the soulless clay giant is a tale that is detailed through intricate paper-cuts.

HONORS

Hush! A Thai Lullaby   Minfong Ho
Illustrated by Holly Meade   Orchard

A strong visual narrative tells the story of a mother who warns a crying mosquito, a leaping frog, and a swinging monkey not to waken her sleeping child. This is a gentle, cumulative bedtime story, sure to please and settle down children.

The Graphic Alphabet David Pelletier Illustrated by the author Orchard

This alphabet book uses computer imagery laced with wit and humor to help young children learn the letters. Each letter is not only represented by a word, image, or concept but also is the word, image, or concept. Crisp imagery is combined with meticulous design.

The Paperboy Dav Pilkey Illustrated by the author Orchard

A boy wakes in the darkness, bundles his newspapers, and accompanied by his faithful dog delivers the daily papers to the still, dark houses. Carefully balanced compositions and a restrained but rich palette give this story tremendous visual appeal.

Starry Messenger: A Book Depicting the Life of a Famous Scientist, Mathematician, Astronomer, Philosopher, Physicist, Galileo Galilei Peter Sís
Illustrated by the author Frances Foster/ Farrar Straus Giroux

Galileo Galilei's story is illustrated in a style that evokes Renaissance art, architecture, and cartography. The events of his everyday life, the struggles and successes, are captured through detailed attention on each page, which brings to life the world on the verge of discovery.

1996 AWARD

Officer Buckle and Gloria Peggy Rathmann
Illustrated by the author Putnam

Police dog Gloria's irreverent acrobatics behind Safety Officer Buckle's back contrast with the officer's straight-laced safety tips to school audiences. Original, lively, and energetic art leads the readers through a story of cooperation and friendship. Watercolor and ink illustrations employ brilliant colors that, combined with a creative use of white space, engage the reader in the humor and warmth of this stellar performance.

HONORS

Alphabet City Stephen T. Johnson Illustrated by the author Viking

Photorealistic paintings of urban environment present an imaginative variety of views and perspectives, textures, and light. Each painting stands alone as a handsome, balanced piece. Together they are an inspiring exercise in seeing patterns and art in everyday things.

Zin! Zin! Zin! a Violin   Lloyd Moss
Illustrated by Marjorie Priceman   Simon & Schuster

> This exuberant introduction to the orchestra is a true celebration of music. The sense of visual musicality is enhanced by warm, changing background colors. The musicians themselves are far from static, and the text has rhythm and punch, changing size and moving across the pages in swoops and swirls to reflect the flow of music.

The Faithful Friend   Robert D. San Souci
Illustrated by Brian Pinkney   Simon & Schuster

> Pinkney's distinctive illustrations evoke the mystery, magic, and romance in San Souci's retelling of this West Indian folktale. The unique scratchboard style, enhanced by vivid oil colors, is a superb match for this atmospheric story in which the main characters confront and ultimately overcome the dark forces of evil.

Tops & Bottoms   Adapted and illustrated by Janet Stevens   Harcourt Brace

> Sleepy, sprawling bear is outwitted by the wily hare, who succeeds in feeding his numerous offspring with abundant vegetable harvests. Handmade vegetable paper and a masterful use of mixed media contribute to this zesty, organic combination of story and illustration.

1995 AWARD

Smoky Night   Eve Bunting   Illustrated by David Diaz   Harcourt Brace

Inspired by the Los Angeles riots, *Smoky Night* relates the happenings of a night of urban rioting from a child's perspective. With thickly textured, expressionistic acrylic paintings set against mixed-media collages, Diaz creates dramatic, groundbreaking illustrations of the night's events. Both language and illustration convey the universal importance of human interaction through the personal story of one little boy and his cat.

HONORS

Swamp Angel   Anne Isaacs   Illustrated by Paul O. Zelinsky   Dutton

> In this original tall tale, Angelica Longrider, known as Swamp Angel, wrestles the huge bear Thundering Tarnation to save the winter supplies of settlers in Tennessee. With his whimsical illustrations, Paul O. Zelinsky has created a memorable heroine with the grit and gusto of a Paul Bunyan. Primitive-style oil paintings on cherry, maple, and birch veneers capture the folksy feel of life in nineteenth-century Tennessee.

John Henry   Julius Lester   Illustrated by Jerry Pinkney   Dial

Pinkney's earthy, craggy pencil and watercolor illustrations capture both the power and the humanity of this African-American folk-hero. Masterful use of light and shadow portray the strength and mass of the Allegheny Mountains, which match the magnitude of John Henry, while delicate shading and mottled color suggest the detail of a realistic natural setting enlivened with touches of whimsy.

Time Flies   Eric Rohmann   Illustrated by the author   Crown

Stunning oil paintings in this wordless picture book dramatically portray a bird's flight though a museum display into the age of the living dinosaurs, where it encounters creatures vastly larger than itself. Rohmann uses rich, realistic shading; texture; and varying perspectives to create the bird's fanciful journey back to the time of its primitive ancestors.

1994 AWARD

Grandfather's Journey   Allen Say   Illustrated by the author   Houghton

Grandfather's Journey eloquently portrays a Japanese immigrant's travels to a new land. Exquisite watercolors portray vast landscapes along with intimate family portraits that communicate hope, dignity, sadness, and love. Say powerfully connects the personal and the universal to create a rare harmony of longing and belonging.

HONORS

Peppe the Lamplighter   Elisa Bartone
Illustrated by Ted Lewin   Lothrop

Lewin vividly captures the bustling market scenes, bleak tenement rooms, and the lamplit streets of turn-of-the-century New York's Little Italy. Dramatic watercolors portray young Peppe's struggle to help support his immigrant family and to win his father's respect.

In the Small, Small Pond   Denise Fleming   Illustrated by the author
Henry Holt

Bright colors and lively language describe the cycle of pond life. Rhyming alliterative text and vibrant illustrations are filled with movement and fun in a joyous celebration of the natural world. Fleming created the illustration by pouring colored pulp through hand-cut stencils.

Owen   Kevin Henkes   Illustrated by the author   Greenwillow

A preschooler mouse, Owen, and his concerned parents confront a classic childhood drama: releasing the trusty, fuzzy blanket. Confident economical line and inspired layout convey Owen's spirited tenacity as he dances toward greater independence.

Raven: A Trickster Tale from the Pacific Northwest
Gerald McDermott   Illustrated by the author   Harcourt Brace Jovanovich

McDermott reshapes the familiar trickster tale from the Pacific Northwest in which Raven steals light from the Sky Chief and brings it to people. Raven's spirit world is boldly colored and hard-edged, a strong graphic contrast to the soft watercolor background of the real Northwest landscape.

Yo! Yes?   Chris Raschka   Illustrated by the author   Orchard

Through bold, original use of line and angle, color and space, Raschka celebrates friendship and offers a timeless message about taking risks. The brief, rhythmic text invites enthusiastic sharing.

1993 AWARD

Mirette on the High Wire   Emily Arnold McCully

Illustrated by the author   Putnam

Emily Arnold McCully's vivid impressionistic watercolors bring nineteenth-century Paris to life with the story of Mirette, a spirited, risk-taking little girl. Mirette enables the former high-wire star Bellini to conquer his fear while achieving her own dream. Light, color, line, and movement in these animated and bold illustrations are in perfect balance with the text.

HONORS

The Stinky Cheese Man & Other Fairly Stupid Tales   Jon Scieszka
Illustrated by Lane Smith   Viking

The Little Red Hen talks in red letters and the giant talks in capitals in this irreverent retelling of the gingerbread man and other time-honored tales. The avant-garde art ("rendered in oil and vinegar" according to the book note) lampoons twentieth-century art in the process. Interdependence of words, visual images, and even the process of book design and publication extract every possible laugh in this outrageous collaboration.

Working Cotton   Sherley Anne Williams
Illustrated by Carole Byard   Harcourt Brace Jovanovich

Carole Byard's dramatic paintings portray the dignity of hard work and the strength of family relationships that are part of this migrant family's life. From the first glimpses of a streaky dawn to the red twilight, powerful, glowing portraits and landscapes poignantly complement the child's poetic depiction of the long workday.

Seven Blind Mice Ed Young Illustrated by the author Philomel

In this successful reinterpretation of the Indian fable of the blind man and the elephant, deceptively simple text integrates concepts of color, numbers, and days of the week with visual irony. Contrasting textured paper heightens the bold color and strong composition, while white typeface against a glossy background and marbleized endpapers add to the excellent design.

1992 AWARD

Tuesday David Wiesner Illustrated by the author Clarion

Flying frogs on lily pads create mischief as they move from the fen to a small town on a Tuesday evening. The story ends with a comic twist suggesting more fantastic flights for the following Tuesday. Wiesner's watercolor illustrations show masterful use of light and dark, alternating perspectives, and variation in page design in this nine-word book.

HONOR

Tar Beach Faith Ringgold Illustrated by the author Crown

Child Cassie flies high above New York City in the 1930s, high above the quilt squares that ground each page, high above the busyness and conflict of everyday life, from family rooftop picnics to daddy's construction work. Acrylic paintings on canvas paper form the basis of this visual feast celebrating the act of transformation, while the quilt form represents a historically important African-American communication medium.

1991 AWARD

Black and White David Macaulay Illustrated by the author Houghton

Macaulay interweaves fantasy and reality in a tale of parents, trains, and cows. The author recommends careful inspection of words and pictures to both minimize and enhance confusion.

HONORS

Puss in Boots Charles Perrault Translated by Malcolm Arthur
Illustrated by Fred Marcellino di Capua/Farrar Straus Giroux

Large pale type and golden-toned paintings work brilliantly together providing an elegant regal look to the familiar fairy tale of Puss. With varied perspectives and

points of view, Marcellino re-creates the French court and countryside to inge-
nious, often droll, effect.

"More, More, More," Said the Baby: 3 Love Stories
Vera B. Williams   Greenwillow

> Brightly framed gouache paintings reflect each child's sense of security and joy as
> a loving adult "catches" that baby up. This creative use of color, shape, and rhythm
> marks a unique and distinctive celebration of family life.

1990 AWARD

Lon Po Po: A Red-Riding Hood Story from China
Ed Young   Translated and illustrated by the author   Philomel

Suspense and drama are lightened with bits of humor as the wolf Lon Po Po tries to
trick three children into letting him into their house. Though he succeeds, the children quickly turn the tables on the wily animal. The artist uses vivid watercolors and
pastels to create dramatic panel pictures.

HONORS

Color Zoo   Lois Ehlert   Illustrated by the author   Lippincott

> Vibrant colors and overlays of geometric-shaped cutouts in heavy paper combine
> to create expressive animal faces. The text is simply a one-word identification of
> the shape or animal. All of the action is in the creative paper engineering.

Hershel and the Hanukkah Goblins   Eric Kimmel
Illustrated by Trina Schart Hyman   Holiday House

> Eight goblins haunt the old synagogue, preventing the villagers from celebrating
> Hanukkah until Hershel arrives to outwit all of the creatures. The dark illustra-
> tions are charged with energy as they show the imaginatively wicked goblins trying
> to frighten Hershel away.

Bill Peet: An Autobiography   Bill Peet   Illustrated by the author   Houghton

> From the time he learned to manipulate a crayon, drawing has been a consum-
> ing passion for Bill Peet. He tells how that passion affected his life, from childhood,
> through his work at the Disney Studios, to his life as an author. Using his usual artis-
> tic style, Peet has filled his autobiography with new black-and-white illustrations.

The Talking Eggs: A Folktale from the American South   Robert D. San Souci
Illustrated by Jerry Pinkney   Dial

> Running away from her angry mother and spoiled sister, Blanche is befriended by
> a strange old woman who owns a cow with two heads and chickens that lay talking

eggs. The eerie and suspenseful black folktale is filled with watercolor pictures of deep woods and strange sights.

1989 AWARD

Song and Dance Man   Karen Ackerman
Illustrated by Stephen Gammell   Knopf

When his grandchildren come to visit, Grandpa whisks them up to the attic, where he performs an exciting vaudeville routine. The colored-pencil sketches are alive with movement and drama.

HONORS

Mirandy and Brother Wind   Patricia C. McKissack
Illustrated by Jerry Pinkney   Knopf

A sparkling, energetic Mirandy vows to dance with the wind at her first cake-walk—but to do that, she must catch it first. Lush, expansive illustrations of the rural South capture the vigor and imagination of the story.

Goldilocks and the Three Bears   Retold and illustrated by James Marshall   Dial

The antithesis of the typical sweet, demure Goldilocks, this little girl with her bouncing golden ringlets is brash, irreverent, and captivating. Set in the present day, the briefly told nursery story abounds with color, humor, and wit.

The Boy of the Three-Year Nap   Diane Snyder
Illustrated by Allen Say   Houghton

Taro has earned his nickname because of his laziness and penchant for sleeping. When he turns trickster to stop his industrious mother's nagging, she in turn outwits him. The handsome pictures are noticeably influenced by eighteenth-century Japanese woodcuts and reflect the culture of the land where this folktale originated.

Free Fall   Illustrated by David Wiesner   Lothrop

In a book made more powerful because it has no words to stifle the imagination, a boy falls asleep and dreams of fantastic adventures. In this visual story, the objects around the boy evolve from one thing into another and then back to their original shapes.

1988 AWARD

Owl Moon   Jane Yolen   Illustrated by John Schoenherr   Philomel

Late one quiet winter's night, a little girl and her father go owling, watching and listening for the signs that say a great horned owl is nearby. Blue-toned color washes and simple landscapes create a frosty, magical night perfect for owl watching.

HONOR

Mufaro's Beautiful Daughters: An African Tale   John Steptoe
Illustrated by the author   Lothrop

> Of the two sisters, one kind and good, the other mean and deceitful, only one will
> be chosen to marry the king. Dramatic yet realistic paintings in lush, jewel-toned
> colors illustrate this folktale from Zimbabwe.

1987 AWARD

Hey, Al   Arthur Yorinks   Illustrated by Richard Egielski
Farrar Straus Giroux

Janitor Al and his dog are swept away from their apparently humdrum lives by a huge
bird that takes them to what at first seems like paradise. Full-color illustrations provide florid scenes of that paradise.

HONORS

The Village of Round and Square Houses   Ann Grifalconi
Illustrated by the author   Little, Brown

> Pastel drawings are used to illustrate the story of the remote Cameron village of
> Tos where the women live in the round houses and the men live in the square ones
> so that each has a place to be together and a place to be apart.

Alphabatics   Suse MacDonald   Illustrated by the author   Bradbury

> Brightly colored letters of the alphabet become acrobats as they twist and turn un-
> til they become the objects that represent the letters: A becomes an ark, J becomes
> a jack-in-the-box, S becomes a swan.

Rumpelstiltskin: From the German of the Brothers Grimm
Retold and illustrated by Paul O. Zelinsky   Dutton

> When the proud father tells the king that his daughter can spin straw into gold,
> it is the tiny Rumpelstiltskin who actually does the spinning—for the price of the
> first-born child. Golden-toned, full-color oil paintings in medieval style retell this
> tale based on an early Brothers Grimm version.

1986 AWARD

The Polar Express   Chris Van Allsburg
Illustrated by the author   Houghton

Dark, brooding illustrations with unusual perspectives set the mood for a magical
and poignant train ride. It is Christmas Eve when the young boy boards the train for
a trip to the North Pole. There he receives a special gift from Santa Claus.

HONORS

The Relatives Came   Cynthia Rylant
Illustrated by Stephen Gammell   Bradbury

> What a marvelous time is had when all the relatives come from Virginia for a visit! They crowd into the house, where there is much loving and hugging and breathing to do together! The pictures nearly bounce off the pages with all the love and happiness in this book.

King Bidgood's in the Bathtub   Audrey Wood
Illustrated by Don Wood   Harcourt

> When the court is in a dither because the king refuses to get out of the bathtub, only the young page knows what to do. Illustrations reminiscent of an opera stage setting show off the full glory of the court scenes.

1985 AWARD

Saint George and the Dragon: A Golden Legend   Adapted from Edmund Spenser's *Faerie Queen* by Margaret Hodges
Illustrated by Trina Schart Hyman   Little, Brown

Lady Una and George, a knight of the Red Cross, must find and battle the terrible dragon that ruins the land. Hyman's illustrations tell the story dramatically, and the reader seems to look at the scenes through an iron-encased window.

HONORS

Hansel and Gretel   Retold by Rika Lesser
Illustrated by Paul O. Zelinsky   Dodd, Mead

> In this book translated from one of the less-embellished versions of the classic Brothers Grimm story, the artwork dominates. Sometimes imitating sixteenth- and seventeenth-century Flemish art, sometimes adopting a romantic nineteenth-century style, the paintings are rich in color and detail.

The Story of Jumping Mouse   Retold and illustrated by John Steptoe   Lothrop

> Large, expressive pencil drawings help tell the tale of a field mouse's search for the Far-Off Land. Armed with courage and hope, the mouse overcomes many obstacles until it is transformed into an eagle. The text is freely adapted from an unidentified Native American "why" story.

Have You Seen My Duckling?   Nancy Tafuri
Illustrated by the author   Greenwillow

> In this almost wordless book, a duck asks the creatures of the pond if they have seen her lost duckling. Bright, clear illustrations show the adventuresome duckling, who is always seen a little hidden from but close to his mother.

1984 AWARD

The Glorious Flight: Across the Channel with Louis Blériot, July 25, 1909
Alice and Martin Provensen   Illustrated by the authors   Viking

Once he sees a flying machine, Louis Blériot becomes passionately interested in building his own machine and is successful on his eleventh attempt. Based on a true incident in France in the early 1900s, the biography is illustrated with pictures of shifting perspectives and touches of humor and views of a family growing older.

HONORS

Ten, Nine, Eight   Molly Bang   Illustrated by the author   Greenwillow

Bedtime becomes a favorite time as the countdown begins. In a lulling rhyme, all of the things in a little girl's room are counted. The quiet time shared between father and daughter is illustrated with warm colors.

Little Red Riding Hood   Retold and illustrated by Trina Schart Hyman
Holiday House

The familiar story of the little girl who goes to visit her grandmother subtly warns children not to talk to strangers. The detailed illustrations seem to place the setting of the story in New England.

1983 AWARD

Shadow   Blaise Cendrars
Translated and illustrated by Marcia Brown   Scribner

Translated from the French poet Blaise Cendrars' work, this symbolic mood piece reflects stories told by African storytellers and shamans around a nighttime fire. Rich colors with black cutout accents create the visual image of the prowling, dancing, mute shadow.

HONORS

When I Was Young in the Mountains   Cynthia Rylant
Illustrated by Diane Goode   Dutton

The author affectionately recalls a childhood spent with her family in the Appalachian Mountains of West Virginia. Warm family scenes are filled with friendly, happy people. Many of the illustrations drift off into the mountain mist and bring a peacefulness to the recalled pleasures.

A Chair for My Mother Vera B. Williams
Illustrated by the author Greenwillow

> After a fire destroys their home, a little girl, her waitress mother, and the girl's grandmother move into an apartment. They start saving all their coins for a big, comfortable chair for Mama and Grandma. The watercolor paintings have a suitably childlike look.

1982 AWARD

Jumanji Chris Van Allsburg Illustrated by the author Houghton

Looking for something to do on a boring afternoon, Peter and Judy decide to try the strange board game they find in the park. Boredom vanishes as every space on which they land comes to life. Meticulously crafted black-and-white illustrations bring the game alive.

HONORS

Where the Buffaloes Begin Olaf Baker
Illustrated by Stephen Gammell Warne

> Majestic, haunting, and moody gray-toned illustrations show Little Wolf on his journey to the sacred place where buffaloes are said to originate. The rich prose was first published in *St. Nicholas Magazine* in 1915.

On Market Street Arnold Lobel Illustrated by Anita Lobel Greenwillow

> A nursery rhyme-like verse breaks into a celebration of all the wares—from A to Z—that a little boy purchases on Market Street. The illustrations, based on seventeenth-century French trade engravings, show brightly colored shopkeepers composed of their merchandise.

Outside over There Maurice Sendak Illustrated by the author Harper & Row

> When Ida is not focusing her complete attention on her baby sister, the baby is kidnapped by hooded goblins and replaced by a baby made of ice. Elaborate paintings combine romantic and surrealistic effects and are filled with subtleties and symbolism.

A Visit to William Blake's Inn: Poems for Innocent and Experienced Travelers
Nancy Willard Illustrated by Alice and Martin Provensen
Harcourt Brace Jovanovich

> Lyrical poems written in the spirit of William Blake combine with captivatingly imaginative illustrations that reflect the staidness and the whimsy of the eighteenth century. Nancy Willard also won the 1982 Newbery Award for this book.

1981 AWARD

Fables   Arnold Lobel   Illustrated by the author   Harper & Row

Twenty original, brief, and witty animal fables, each complete with a moral, expose human foibles. Each fable is faced with a full-page painting in soft, rich colors that show the droll animals at the crucial moment of the fable.

HONORS

The Grey Lady and the Strawberry Snatcher   Molly Bang
Illustrated by the author   Four Winds

An old lady who, except for her hands and face, appears as a grey silhouette, buys a basket of strawberries and proceeds home, pursued by a strawberry snatcher. Interesting colors and textures are effectively combined with negative grey shapes in this vivid visual hide-and-seek game.

Truck   Donald Crews   Illustrated by the author   Greenwillow

Bright colors and geometric shapes roll across the pages as a truck carries a cargo of tricycles to its destination. There is no text. From the loading dock, through intricate highway systems, past road signs, to a truck stop, in clear and stormy weather, the big red truck moves its precious cargo across the country.

Mice Twice   Joseph Low   Illustrated by the author
Margaret K. McElderry/Atheneum

Cat is very hungry and wants a nice tender mouse to eat, so he invites Mouse to dinner. Things escalate until even Lion and Crocodile are involved. It is Wasp who settles things in this funny tale that is enhanced through whimsical drawings.

The Bremen-Town Musicians   Retold and illustrated by Ilse Plume   Doubleday

Four animals, all unwanted, set out together to become musicians but instead end up outwitting a band of robbers. The Brothers Grimm tale is illustrated with glowing, subdued colors and rounded shapes.

1980 AWARD

Ox-Cart Man   Donald Hall   Illustrated by Barbara Cooney   Viking

Clean, uncluttered paintings capture the flavor of nineteenth-century New England as a family's day-to-day life is mandated by the changing season. There is a strong sense of the passage of time and rhythm of life in this book.

HONORS

Ben's Trumpet   Rachel Isadora   Illustrated by the author   Greenwillow/Morrow

> The mood, sounds, and rhythms of jazz pulsate through the illustrations as Ben sits on the fire escape and blows his imaginary trumpet to the jazz sounds emanating from the Zig Zig Jazz Club. Set in the twenties and illustrated with dynamic black-and-white drawings, this is the story of one boy's dream coming true.

The Treasure   Uri Shulevitz   Illustrated by the author   Farrar Straus Giroux

> A poor man dreams that he must go to the castle bridge and wait for something that will turn about his fortunes. Traveling far to get there, he learns that the treasure is under his own stove. Illustrations with softly glowing colors and a striking use of light depict traditional eastern European villages and countrysides.

The Garden of Abdul Gasazi   Chris Van Allsburg
Illustrated by the author   Houghton

> Illusion and reality become blurred when the unruly dog the boy has been tending runs away into the secret, foreboding garden of a retired magician. The visual perspectives and the play of light on the gray pencil drawings create an eerie, mysterious feeling.

1979 AWARD

The Girl Who Loved Wild Horses   Paul Goble
Illustrated by the author   Bradbury

The kinship is so strong between a Plains Indian girl and the horses she has lived with since becoming lost in a storm, that eventually she becomes one of them. Sharp, brilliantly colored paintings sweep across the pages and are in perfect harmony with the story.

HONORS

Freight Train   Donald Crews   Illustrated by the author   Greenwillow/Morrow

> Large pictures of the different freight cars are identified by name and by color. Soon the train begins to move into a blur of colors as it swiftly goes on its way.

The Way to Start a Day   Byrd Baylor   Illustrated by Peter Parnall   Scribner

> A vibrant sunflower yellow and other colors blend with crisp, black lines to make effective use of symbolism in celebration of the sun. Poetic prose tells how cultures throughout the ages have sung to the new day's sun to honor it.

1978 AWARD

Noah's Ark   Peter Spier   Illustrated by the author   Doubleday

The only text is the seventeenth-century Dutch poem, "The Flood," by Jacobus Revius, that opens the book. The rest of the book is a visual interpretation of Noah and his unbelievably difficult task of tending the animals on the ark. Careful details and softly hued watercolors depict the story with reverence, humor, and delight.

HONORS

Castle   David Macaulay   Illustrated by the author   Houghton

> Macaulay traces in text and drawings the step-by-step construction of a fictitious thirteenth-century English castle in Wales from its conception to its baptism by fire—a direct attack by hundreds of Welsh soldiers. The complex engineering task is generously illustrated with detailed black-and-white line drawings and diagrams.

It Could Always Be Worse: A Yiddish Folktale   Retold and illustrated by Margot Zemach   Farrar Straus Giroux

> Crowded into one room with his mother, wife, and six children, a man goes to the rabbi for help. The rabbi's answer is to bring one animal after another to live in the house. Dynamic, earth-toned paintings with an eastern European look capture the humor of the rabbi's good advice.

1977 AWARD

Ashanti to Zulu: African Traditions   Margaret Musgrove
Illustrated by Leo and Diane Dillon   Dial

Twenty-six different African tribal traditions and customs are introduced using the English alphabet as the vehicle. A border on each page frames the text and illustrations, where glowing colors mix with rich browns. The attention to authentic detail in each painting is remarkable.

HONORS

Hawk, I'm Your Brother   Byrd Baylor   Illustrated by Peter Parnall   Scribner

> In a gentle story told in simple, poetic prose, a young Native American boy wants desperately to fly like a hawk. Spacious, clean, panoramic line drawings convey the yearning of the boy and the power of the hawk.

Fish for Supper M. B. Goffstein Illustrated by the author Dial

> This quiet story chronicles the simple daily routine of Grandma, whose life centers around fishing. The black-and-white line drawings are centered in a square border of white space.

The Contest Retold and illustrated by Nonny Hogrogian Greenwillow/Morrow

> Realizing that they are both engaged to the same woman and each unwilling to give her up, two robbers compare their cleverness in thievery to see who deserves her. Large, colorful illustrations capture the flavor of the Armenian culture in this humorous folktale.

The Golem Beverly Brodsky McDermott Illustrated by the author Lippincott

> The somber Jewish legend of the Golem, a creature created from clay that becomes more powerful and terrible than the evil he was made to destroy, is re-created with high visual drama. Striking paintings, vibrant with deep, rich colors, are filled with symbolism and massive shapes.

The Amazing Bone William Steig Illustrated by the author
Farrar Straus Giroux

> On her way home from school, hapless heroine Pearl Pig finds an amazing talking bone. When the delectable piglet is waylaid by a debonair fox, the amazing bone saves Pearl. Sunny, fresh, springtime landscapes provide the background for the well-dressed characters.

1976 AWARD

Why Mosquitoes Buzz in People's Ears: A West African Tale
Retold by Verna Aardema Illustrated by Leo and Diane Dillon Dial

Mosquito tells Iguana a tall tale about yams that annoys Iguana so much that he puts sticks in his ears so he cannot hear such things. Thus begins a chain reaction tale of the West African jungle. Illustrations show highly stylized animals.

HONORS

The Desert Is Theirs Byrd Baylor Illustrated by Peter Parnall Scribner

> A spare, lyrical text tells of the relationship of the Papagos people to their environment—"we share . . . we only share." The paintings are dramatic and are reminiscent of the layers of colors found in sand paintings.

Strega Nona: An Old Tale   Tomie dePaola
Illustrated by the author   Prentice-Hall

> Strega Nona leaves Big Anthony alone with her magic pasta pot after telling him never to touch it. It is not long before he does, and pasta literally flows through the town. Characters in medieval costumes of pastel, jewel-like colors add to the humor of the story.

1975 AWARD

Arrow to the Sun: A Pueblo Indian Tale   Gerald McDermott
Adapted and Illustrated by the author   Viking

The son of the Lord of the Sun sets out to find his father in this adaptation of a Pueblo legend. On his way, he undergoes four trials to prove his relationship to the Sun. The stylized, strong geometric art vividly portrays the desert and its intense sun colors.

HONOR

Jambo Means Hello: Swahili Alphabet Book   Muriel Feelings
Illustrated by Tom Feelings   Dial

> Letters of the alphabet are represented by words of the Swahili language. A brief explanation of the word includes cultural information of East African countries. Beautiful full-page illustrations further depict the cultures.

1974 AWARD

Duffy and the Devil: A Cornish Tale   Retold by Harve Zemach
Illustrated by Margot Zemach   Farrar Straus Giroux

The Cornish version of Rumpelstiltskin has delightful twists. When the maid guesses the devil's name, everything that he has sewn turns to ashes. Lightly colored illustrations treat the story with grand humor, and at the instant the name is guessed, the Squire is left standing in the fields, naked except for hat and shoes.

HONORS

Three Jovial Huntsmen   Adapted and illustrated by Susan Jeffers   Bradbury

> The three jovial huntsmen go a-hunting on St. David's day and find nothing they want. But lurking in the beautifully drawn forests, many animals are seen keeping a close watch on the huntsmen.

Cathedral: The Story of Its Construction   David Macaulay
Illustrated by the author   Houghton

> The single-mindedness and spirit of the people and their step-by-step construction of an imaginary medieval cathedral are meticulously recorded as the author-illustrator celebrates the lives and art of the craftsmen who built the magnificent Gothic cathedrals.

1973 AWARD

The Funny Little Woman   Retold by Arlene Mosel
Illustrated by Blair Lent   Dutton

A little woman pursues a rice dumpling and is led into the underground world of the wicked Oni. Her escape proves she is a funny little woman. Illustrations convey the mystery and humor of the strange world of the Oni as well as the dignity of this Japanese folktale.

HONORS

Hosie's Alphabet   Hosea, Tobias, and Lisa Baskin
Illustrated by Leonard Baskin   Viking

> From the bumptious baboon, to the primordial protozoa, right down to the "ruminating zebu," the artist presents an alphabet bestiary of ever-changing format where spiders' legs stretch across the page and dashes of watercolor become the eagle. This work is highly imaginative.

When Clay Sings   Byrd Baylor   Illustrated by Tom Bahti   Scribner

> Illustrated with the designs found on prehistoric pottery from the American Southwest, this tribute to artifacts and those who used them evokes a reverence for an ancient way of life. The earth tones and prehistoric designs dignify the word images of the poetic text.

Snow-White and the Seven Dwarfs: A Tale from the Brothers Grimm
Translated by Randall Jarrell   Illustrated by Nancy Ekholm Burkert
Farrar Straus Giroux

> Strongly detailed illustrations in beautiful, soft colors evoke the sweeping, medieval, magical romance of fairy tales. Randall Jarrell translated the Brothers Grimm story of the beautiful girl, the wicked, malicious stepmother, and the sturdy, somber dwarfs.

Anansi the Spider: A Tale from the Ashanti
Adapted and illustrated by Gerald McDermott   Holt Rinehart & Winston

> The moon is in the sky because Anansi, the great African folklore hero, could not decide which of his six sons should have it. Bright, geometric designs, bold, stylized animals, and rhythmic speech patterns are based on the Ashanti culture.

1972 AWARD

One Fine Day   Retold and illustrated by Nonny Hogrogian   Macmillan

Punished by having his tail cut off when he drank all the milk in an old woman's pail, the fox pleads to have it sewn back on so his friends won't make fun of him. The old woman agrees to do it, but only after he has returned her milk. The subdued and uncluttered pictures reflect the humorous cumulative action of the Armenian tale.

HONORS

If All the Seas Were One Sea   Janina Domanska
Illustrated by the author   Macmillan

> An old nursery rhyme, its rise-and-fall rhythmic text reminiscent of the action of ocean waves, is treated to splendid etchings boldly filled with swirling, geometric lines of clear colors. The many shapes of each etching make a whole picture and provide the rhyme with even more momentum.

Moja Means One: Swahili Counting Book   Muriel Feelings
Illustrated by Tom Feelings   Dial

> Numbers from one to ten are represented by words in the Swahili language. Handsome, muted-gray double-page spread paintings depict scenes from Africa and relate to the illustrative sentences.

Hildilid's Night   Cheli Durán Ryan   Illustrated by Arnold Lobel   Macmillan

> Hildilid hates the night and the creatures of it. She does everything she can to chase the night away. Pen-and-ink drawings composed of thousands of tiny lines add a moonlit quality to the pages. Only at the end, with the approach of dawn, does yellow come into the picture.

1971 AWARD

A Story a Story: An African Tale
Retold and illustrated by Gail E. Haley   Atheneum

Kwaku Ananse, the great African spider man, completes three almost impossible tasks to win the Sky God's box of stories to tell throughout the world. The woodcut illustrations use African designs.

HONORS

Frog and Toad Are Friends   Arnold Lobel   Illustrated by the author
Harper & Row

> In five affectionate and funny stories, best friends Frog and Toad share simple adventures and experiences. They welcome spring, find a lost button, tell stories, and enjoy being friends. The expressive and droll illustrations are in gray, frog green, and toad brown.

In the Night Kitchen   Maurice Sendak   Illustrated by the author   Harper & Row

> Falling through the night and out of his clothes, Mickey lands in cake batter in the night kitchen. From there he goes to the dough, builds an airplane of it, and flies to the Milky Way. The dream-fantasy is carried out in a chanting rhyme and is illustrated with an adaptation of comic book art.

The Angry Moon   Retold by William Sleator   Illustrated by Blair Lent
Atlantic/Little, Brown

> A legend of the peoples of Alaska is retold with vigor, using lavish, full-color illustrations that elaborate on original Tlingit motifs. When Lapowinsa mocks the moon, she is taken into the sky country. Her friend must overcome many obstacles before he is able to rescue her.

1970 AWARD

Sylvester and the Magic Pebble   William Steig
Illustrated by the author   Windmill/Simon & Schuster

A collector of pebbles, Sylvester the donkey finds a magic one that grants wishes. Caught by a lion, Sylvester panics and wishes himself to be a rock. Full-color pictures show the seasonal changes and colorful characters of the story and extend its concern and gentle humor.

HONORS

Goggles!   Ezra Jack Keats   Illustrated by the author   Macmillan

> While showing off the motorcycle goggles he has found, Peter is accosted by neighborhood bullies. Proving that smart moves are more powerful than brute strength, Peter and his friends outwit the older boys. Rich, dark, brooding colors of paint and collage are lightened with vibrant colors in illustrations that reflect the urban setting.

Alexander and the Wind-Up Mouse   Leo Lionni
Illustrated by the author   Pantheon

> Alexander, an unappreciated house mouse, envies Willy the windup mouse because everyone loves and coddles him. After asking the wizard lizard to change him into a windup mouse, Alexander has a change of heart. Large, bold collages enhance the simply told story.

Pop Corn and Ma Goodness   Edna Mitchell Preston
Illustrated by Robert Andrew Parker   Viking

> With all the gaiety and drama of a folk song, this original story is told in nonsense verse. Ma Goodness and Pop Corn meet, fall in love, marry, build a house and a farm, have children, and enjoy the good life on their "prippitty proppetty." Watercolor pictures have a haphazard look that adds to the rollicking fun.

Thy Friend, Obadiah   Brinton Turkle   Illustrated by the author   Viking

> His large Quaker family teases young Obadiah because a sea gull has taken a liking to him and follows him everywhere. The drawings are warm and gentle and vary greatly in perspective. When the sea gull fails to be seen for several days, Obadiah finds that what he thought was a nuisance is really a friend.

The Judge: An Untrue Tale   Harve Zemach
Illustrated by Margot Zemach   Farrar Straus Giroux

> Prisoner after prisoner excitedly tells the Judge about the horrible thing that is on its way. The no-nonsense Judge throws them all in jail. When the horrible thing comes, poetic justice is done. Illustrated in watercolors and line drawings, the robust, pinkish characters tell their cumulative rhyming tale.

1969 AWARD

The Fool of the World and the Flying Ship: A Russian Tale
Retold by Arthur Ransome   Illustrated by Uri Shulevitz
Farrar Straus Giroux

Line drawings and watercolors in bright, glowing, jewel-toned colors show the magnificent flying ship and the landscapes and onion domes of Russia. In this old Russian tale, the scorned and foolish younger son of peasants overcomes tremendous obstacles and wins the hand of the czar's daughter.

HONOR

Why the Sun and the Moon Live in the Sky   Elphinstone Dayrell
Illustrated by Blair Lent   Houghton

> Long ago, so the Nigerian folktale says, the Sun and Water were friends and lived on Earth together. When Sun invites Water to visit, the resulting flood forces them

into the sky. Elaborately stylized African motifs and traditional patterns are used throughout the book.

1968 AWARD

Drummer Hoff   Adapted by Barbara Emberley
Illustrated by Ed Emberley   Prentice-Hall

"Private Parridge brought the carriage," begins the cumulative text that leads to "Drummer Hoff fired it off" and a big "Kahbahblooom." Woodcuts show vibrantly colored old-fashioned military figures.

HONORS

Frederick   Leo Lionni   Illustrated by the author   Pantheon

The other field mice scurry to gather food for winter while Frederick gathers warm thoughts. In the deep of winter when the food has run out, Frederick is called upon to share his supplies. Collages enhance this story that proves "we do not live by bread alone."

Seashore Story   Taro Yashima   Illustrated by the author   Viking

On an island where "the quietness of ancient times" is felt, visiting children are reminded of the old story of Urashima, a fisherman who saved the life of a turtle. In return, the turtle takes him deep into the ocean to a mythical land. Muted pastel drawings capture the mysticism of the Japanese story.

The Emperor and the Kite   Jane Yolen   Illustrated by Ed Young   World

Djeow Seow was the smallest and least noticed of the emperor's children. When evil men come and snatch the emperor away, it is Djeow Seow with her kites who rescues him. Intricate paper cuttings provide great beauty and a sense of cultural heritage in this Japanese tale.

1967 AWARD

Sam, Bangs & Moonshine   Evaline Ness   Illustrated by the author
Holt Rinehart & Winston

Sam, a fisherman's daughter, has a bad habit of making up stories. The little girl learns to distinguish the truth from "moonshine" only after her best friend and her cat nearly meet tragedy. The book's pictures capture Sam's confusion of fact and fancy.

HONOR

One Wide River to Cross Adapted by Barbara Emberley
Illustrated by Ed Emberley Prentice-Hall

> The text of an old folk song comes alive on brightly colored pages printed with black woodcuts. Stylized animals come forth one by one, two by two, and so on up to ten in nonsense verse with illustrations of animals that cumulate in groups waiting to board Noah's ark.

1966 AWARD

Always Room for One More Sorche Nic Leodhas, pseud. (Leclaire Alger) Illustrated by Nonny Hogrogian Holt Rinehart & Winston

A man invites all passersby to share his house with his wife and ten children until the house finally bursts apart. The Scottish folk song is told in lilting verse and illustrated in a subdued, dreamy manner.

HONORS

Just Me Marie Hall Ets Illustrated by the author Viking

> The little boy tries to imitate the hops, walks, and wiggles of the animals on his farm. But when he sees his father, he runs to him as only he can run. Black-and-white drawings have a charming rhythmic expression.

Tom Tit Tot Retold and illustrated by Evaline Ness Scribner

> In this English variant of Rumpelstiltskin, the heroine is a comic, homespun character. Woodcuts executed in brown, gold, black, and aqua capture the broad humor and Elizabethan tone of the story.

Hide and Seek Fog Alvin Tresselt Illustrated by Roger Duvoisin Lothrop

> As thick fog settles down for a stay, the lobstermen cannot put out to sea, the vacationers grumble because they cannot do anything, and the children frolic and play hide-and-seek. Pictures and text describe how life becomes transformed in a dense, wet, lingering fog on the Atlantic seacoast.

1965 AWARD

May I Bring a Friend? Beatrice Schenk de Regniers
Illustrated by Beni Montresor Atheneum

Invited to tea by the king and queen each day of one week, the child quite naturally asks if he can bring a friend with him. Each day he brings animals from the zoo, and not all are well behaved! In rhymed text and creative illustrations reminiscent of stage settings, the absurd story is told.

HONORS

A Pocketful of Cricket   Rebecca Caudill   Illustrated by Evaline Ness
Holt Rinehart & Winston

> One day a boy who delights in the countryside finds a cricket and takes it home for a pet. An understanding teacher shows him how to share his special love of the cricket with the whole class. Pictures portray the inquisitiveness of a young farm boy.

The Wave   Margaret Hodges   Adapted from Lafacdio Hearn's *Gleanings in Buddha-Fields*   Illustrated by Blair Lent   Houghton

> Giisan, the wise and respected old man of the Japanese village, must act quickly to warn the villagers that they are in great danger. The relentlessness of the tidal wave is seen in the brown, gold, gray, and black prints on every page and is heard in the urgency with which the story is told.

Rain Makes Applesauce   Julian Scheer   Illustrated by Marvin Bileck
Holiday House

> Each two-page spread contains a nonsense line that always ends with "And rain makes applesauce" and the accusation, "Oh you're just talking silly talk." Illustrations in rich but delicate colors have an almost surrealistic effect and add a sophisticated tone.

1964 AWARD

Where the Wild Things Are   Maurice Sendak
Illustrated by the author   Harper & Row

Sent to bed without any supper, Max travels far to where the wild things are. Taming them with a special magic trick, Max suddenly longs to be at home. The pictures are full of movement and magic, and in several two-page spreads without text they are absolutely boisterous.

HONORS

Swimmy   Leo Lionni   Illustrated by the author   Pantheon

> Swimmy, a small, black fish, convinces a school of small fish to swim in the formation of a large fish, thus proving that in numbers there is strength. The watery world is filled with shapes, patterns, and colors.

All in the Morning Early   Sorche Nic Leodhas, pseud. (Leclaire Alger)
Illustrated by Evaline Ness   Holt Rinehart & Winston

> Asked by his mother to take a sack of corn to the mill, Sandy starts on his way. With each animal or person he meets along the way, the cumulative rhythmic tale grows longer. The drawings, with their overlapping colors, place the scene in Scotland, where the old rhyme originated.

Mother Goose and Nursery Rhymes   Illustrated by Philip Reed   Atheneum

> Wood engravings, both serious and silly in approach, decorate nearly all sixty-six rhymes and proverbs included in this collection. Large print, generous margins, crisp and colorful engravings, and just one or two nursery rhymes a page encourage a lingering look at each illustration.

1963 AWARD

The Snowy Day   Ezra Jack Keats   Illustrated by the author   Viking

Peter has fun on a snow-covered day making tracks and angels in the snow, building a snowman, and even trying to save a snowball for later. Spare, colorful collage pictures capture the wonder of a small child's trudge through new snow.

HONORS

The Sun Is a Golden Earring   Natalia M. Belting
Illustrated by Bernarda Bryson   Holt Rinehart & Winston

> People have always wondered about nature and have made up stories and sayings to explain natural phenomena. The author's collection of ancient sayings from folklore is reproduced here. The drawings lend an effective ethereal spirit to the book.

Mr. Rabbit and the Lovely Present   Charlotte Zolotow
Illustrated by Maurice Sendak   Harper & Row

> A little girl seeks birthday present advice from the wonderfully lanky, long-legged Mr. Rabbit. As the two wander through beautiful pastel scenes, she explains that her mother likes colors. They discuss many objects that are of the colors her mother likes the best.

1962 AWARD

Once a Mouse . . . A Fable   Retold and illustrated
by Marcia Brown   Scribner

The brief, carefully chosen text taken from a fable of ancient India tells of a hermit magician that changes a mouse into a cat, a dog, a tiger, and finally back into a mouse again. Illustrated in woodcuts filled with patterns, the overlaying of the gold, red, and black add even more dimension.

HONORS

The Day We Saw the Sun Come Up   Alice E. Goudey
Illustrated by Adrienne Adams   Scribner

> In this poetic science book, two children get up very early in the morning and see the sun come up. They watch their long shadows and see what happens to them later in the day. Illustrations are in appropriate colors—gray and shadowy in the early morning, bright and clear at noon.

Little Bear's Visit   Else Holmelund Minarik
Illustrated by Maurice Sendak   Harper & Row

> Little Bear thoroughly enjoys his visit with his grandparents and delights in the stories they tell. The brown, green, and black-and-white illustrations of the cuddly, loving Little Bear and his fully clothed grandparents are enhanced with fine crosshatching.

The Fox Went Out on a Chilly Night: An Old Song
Illustrated by Peter Spier   Doubleday

> Alternating double-page spreads of full-color and black-and-white detailed drawings greatly extend the story told in the old song. The fox kills a duck and a goose, outruns the farmer, and dines with his wife with fork and knife while the ten little pups chew on the "bones-o." The musical score is appended.

1961 AWARD

Baboushka and the Three Kings   Adapted from a Russian Folk Tale
Ruth Robbins   Illustrated by Nicolas Sidjakov   Parnassus

Old Baboushka declined to go with the three kings in search of the Child. Now, every year at Christmastime she continues her endless, endless search. On her way she leaves gifts for children. Rich, four-color, angular pictures in primitive style adorn the Russian tale.

HONOR

Inch by Inch   Leo Lionni   Illustrated by the author   Obolensky

> An inchworm saves himself from being eaten because he is able to measure things—a robin's tail, a flamingo's neck, a hummingbird's body. But when asked to measure the nightingale's song, the inchworm must think fast. The bright green inchworm inches its way out of sight through a collage of grass.

1960 AWARD

Nine Days to Christmas Marie Hall Ets and Aurora Labastida
Illustrated by Marie Hall Ets Viking

Now that she is in kindergarten, Ceci is old enough to join in the posadas—part of the special Christmas celebration that begins nine days before Christmas. Anticipation mounts as Ceci chooses her own piñata. Soft, gray backgrounds with splashes of bright colors project the warmth and excitement of the Mexican tradition in an urban setting.

HONORS

Houses from the Sea Alice E. Goudey
Illustrated by Adrienne Adams Scribner

Soft watercolor washes combine with poetic text to set the tone of this quiet, informative story. Two children gather shells along the coast and talk about the various shapes of the shells. An introduction and afterword provide more scientific information.

The Moon Jumpers Janice May Udry Illustrated by Maurice Sendak
Harper & Row

When the sun goes down, the moon comes up. Four children calling themselves the moon jumpers joyfully play and dance under the moonlit sky before bedtime. Soft night colors add a mystic touch to the simple story.

1959 AWARD

Chanticleer and the Fox Geoffrey Chaucer
Adapted and illustrated by Barbara Cooney Crowell

The old fable of the proud rooster and the wily fox was retold by Chaucer in his *Canterbury Tales.* Cooney has adapted that version for children. The text is filled with descriptive language, while the illustrations, rich in color and strong lines, capture medieval times.

HONORS

The House That Jack Built/La Maison Que Jacques A Batie
Antonio Frasconi Illustrated by the author Harcourt Brace

An old cumulative nursery rhyme, told in English and French, is illustrated with brilliantly colored woodcuts. A review at the end of the text asks questions in English and provides answers in French.

What Do You Say, Dear? Sesyle Joslin
Illustrated by Maurice Sendak   Young Scott

> Absurdly funny and outlandish situations are presented, followed by the question, "what do you say, dear?" and the proper rule of etiquette. Blue, yellow, and black illustrations continue the hilarity, even though the rule is presented straightforwardly.

Umbrella Taro Yashima   Illustrated by the author   Viking

> Thrilled with the umbrella and red boots she receives on her third birthday, Momo impatiently waits out the days until it rains. How proud she is when she can finally use her new rain gear! The impressionistic illustrations are filled with brush strokes of red, blues, and yellows and reflect the Japanese culture.

1958 AWARD

Time of Wonder Robert McCloskey   Illustrated by the author   Viking

McCloskey celebrates in prose and painting the island where he lives. The alternately quiet and boisterous moods of nature are peacefully or dramatically recounted. The children of the island explore and enjoy the changing moods as the intensity of the blue and green watercolors shifts with the changes in the weather.

HONORS

Fly High, Fly Low Don Freeman   Illustrated by the author   Viking

> In a story of love, loyalty, and suspense, the pigeon Sid faces perils while searching for the missing Midge, their nest, and the big letter B where their nest is housed. Colorful illustrations reveal scenes of San Francisco.

Anatole and the Cat Eve Titus   Illustrated by Paul Galdone   McGraw-Hill

> Mouse Anatole, a loving husband and caring father, bicycles through the streets of Paris each night on his way to work. When a cat arrives on the scene, Anatole succeeds where thousands of other mice have failed. Gray drawings with accents of red, white, and blue and a smattering of French words reinforce the setting of the story.

1957 AWARD

A Tree Is Nice Janice May Udry   Illustrated by Marc Simont   Harper

Trees are wonderful: They give shade, are fun to climb, are great to swing from, and even give cats a place to hide from dogs. Illustrated with watercolors, this book is a celebration of trees.

HONORS

Gillespie and the Guards   Benjamin Elkin
Illustrated by James Daugherty   Viking

> Gillespie sets out to fool the three haughty guards by the old trick of the obvious. Robust illustrations are filled with humor and point with pride to the little boy who outsmarts the smug guards.

Lion   William Pène du Bois   Illustrated by the author   Viking

> High in the sky, in the place where animals are invented, the boss comes up with a wonderful new name for an animal—"lion." His difficulty in deciding what it should look like is depicted in a line drawing of his original idea of a lion, complete with feathers, fur, and fish scales.

Mr. Penny's Race Horse   Marie Hall Ets   Illustrated by the author   Viking

> Mr. Penny promises his animals a ride on the Ferris wheel if they win enough prize money at the fair. In an attempt to make sure they win first prize, the animals cause chaos. The dark black-and-white illustrations of the farm and the fair are all set within a border.

Anatole   Eve Titus   Illustrated by Paul Galdone   McGraw-Hill

> Shocked and shaken when he overhears humans saying that mice are terrible and dirty, Anatole the mouse determines to give humans something in return for the food he takes. Red, white, blue, and gray illustrations alternate with black-and-white ones as they reveal the world from the perspective of a French mouse.

1 Is One   Tasha Tudor   Illustrated by the author   Oxford

> Simple verse and delicate old-fashioned paintings and drawings introduce numerals from one to twenty. Each page is bordered with charming drawings of wild flowers. Within the borders children and scenes from nature represent the number depicted.

1956 AWARD

Frog Went A-Courtin'   Retold by John Langstaff
Illustrated by Feodor Rojankovsky   Harcourt Brace

In this story based on an old song and written in snappy, rhyming couplets, a frog courts Miss Mousie, and soon the insects and small animals scurry about preparing for the wedding feast. Full-color illustrations alternate with black-and-white and frog green ones, climaxing in a state of confusion as the cat joins the feast. Music is included.

HONORS

Play with Me   Marie Hall Ets   Illustrated by the author   Viking

> Reaching out to touch the woodland animals that she wants to play with, the little girl finds that they all run from her. She sits very still, and one by one the animals come close to her. Repetition in the story is loosely carried out in the quiet drawings as the girl never strays far from the pond.

Crow Boy   Taro Yashima   Illustrated by the author   Viking

> In a deeply sensitive school story, Chibi, a very shy boy, is taunted by his classmates for years. A new teacher takes the time to talk to Chibi and discovers his talents. Set in a Japanese village, the story is illustrated with brush strokes that reflect an economy of style.

1955 AWARD

Cinderella, or the Little Glass Slipper
Illustrated and translated from the French of Charles Perrault
by Marcia Brown   Scribner

Freely translated from Charles Perrault's French tale, this story of Cinderella, her ugly stepsisters, the fairy godmother, and the glass slipper is enhanced with illustrations that fairly dance across the pages with pink and aqua colors and whispy black lines. The enchanting pictures capture the romance of the tale.

HONORS

Wheel on the Chimney   Margaret Wise Brown
Illustrated by Tibor Gergely   Lippincott

> Storks come from Africa to build their nest on the chimney and live by the cool, green rivers of Hungary. When fall comes they fly south over towns, rivers, and bridges. The full-page paintings of the Mediterranean city, the pink flamingos, and the flock of white storks in flight are striking in color.

The Thanksgiving Story   Alice Dalgliesh   Illustrated by Helen Sewell   Scribner

> Events leading up to the first Thanksgiving celebration in Plymouth Colony are told with the Hopkins family as the focus. Flat, primitive color illustrations of people are interspersed with rust-colored silhouettes of objects important to the Pilgrims in their new land.

Book of Nursery and Mother Goose Rhymes   Illustrated by Marguerite de Angeli
Doubleday

> Three hundred seventy-six rhymes are delicately illustrated in this oversized book. A soft, cheerful tone pervades the sketches, many of which were inspired

by scenes of the English countryside. A small sketch of a goose appears on almost every page.

1954 AWARD

Madeline's Rescue Ludwig Bemelmans
Illustrated by the author Viking

When Madeline is rescued from the river by a dog, the dog becomes the heroine of the convent school. The girls love the dog, but the trustees say it must go. Bright, irrepressible pictures match the indomitable spirit of the little French girl.

HONORS

The Steadfast Tin Soldier Hans Christian Andersen
Translated by M. R. James Illustrated by Marcia Brown Scribner

Five-and-twenty tin soldiers, all made from the same tin spoon, look alike except for the last one made. He stands firmly on his one leg. It is he who falls in love with the toy ballerina. Their tragic story is enhanced with blue-violet and red drawings.

Green Eyes Abe Birnbaum Illustrated by the author Capitol

An all-white cat with long whiskers and green eyes is about to celebrate his first birthday. In simple text and drawings reminiscent of the bold lines of children's art, the tale of Green Eyes's activities in the four seasons that have just passed unfolds.

A Very Special House Ruth Krauss Illustrated by Maurice Sendak Harper

The little boy is blissfully happy as he tells of a house he knows where he puts his feet on the table, bounces on the bed, and swings on the door. It is a place where everyone yells for more, and no one ever says "stop." Line illustrations seem to frolic across the page, and only at the end is it revealed that the story is a triumph of imaginary play.

Journey Cake, Ho! Ruth Sawyer Illustrated by Robert McCloskey Viking

When there is only enough food left to feed two, not three, the bound-out boy is sent on his way with a huge Journey Cake. The cake breaks free, bounces down the road, and soon animal after animal joins the chase until they all end up where the boy started. Expressive illustrations provide the feel of an American folktale.

When Will the World Be Mine? The Story of a Snowshoe Rabbit Miriam Schlein
Illustrated by Jean Charlot W. R. Scott

Little Snowshoe Rabbit is born in the spring. His mother spends much of the year protecting and teaching him. She gently shows him how to adapt to the world around him, and in that way the world becomes his. The lithographs in browns and greens show stylized rabbits and their view of the world.

1953 AWARD

The Biggest Bear   Lynd Ward   Illustrated by the author   Houghton

Humiliated because his family has the only barn that never has a bear skin hanging on it, Johnny sets out with his shotgun in search of a bear. He returns home with a live, cuddly, hungry bear cub that soon grows into a big, rambunctious, voracious bear. The illustrations are sensitive, strong, and robust.

HONORS

Ape in a Cape: An Alphabet of Odd Animals   Fritz Eichenberg
Illustrated by the author   Harcourt Brace

Bold, humorous, colorful pictures and short, nonsense verses combine to create a lively alphabet book. From the "bear in despair" to the "yak with a pack," there is wonderful fun and imagination on each page.

Five Little Monkeys   Juliet Kepes   Illustrated by the author   Houghton

Buzzo, Binki, Bulu, Bibi, and Bali are the little mischievous monkeys who, because of their irritating tricks, cause the other jungle animals to band together to punish them. Alternating pages of color and black-and-white illustrations show the stylized monkeys acting up.

One Morning in Maine   Robert McCloskey   Illustrated by the author   Viking

While clam digging with her father, Sally loses a tooth that falls amongst the pebbles of the beach. Large, dark blue lithographs depict the great pride associated with losing the first baby tooth. All the characters in the small Maine town enjoy Sally's joy.

Puss in Boots   Translated and illustrated from Charles Perrault
by Marcia Brown   Scribner

The youngest son inherits a cat and realizes that after eating it he will have nothing left. Crafty Puss in Boots tells his master to do as he says and all will be well, and indeed it is! Puss, with his fine red boots, is shown as a grand, swashbuckling character who takes command of all the folderol of a French court.

The Storm Book   Charlotte Zolotow
Illustrated by Margaret Bloy Graham   Harper

A little boy watches in wonder as the day turns ominously gray and still, a storm approaches, and breaks forth. He asks his mother questions and she replies with reassuring answers. Each two-page spread of text is followed by a double-page spread of illustrations, most of them showing a driving rain.

1952 AWARD

Finders Keepers Will, pseud. (William Lipkind)
Illustrated by Nicolas, pseud. (Nicolas Mordvinoff) Harcourt Brace

Two dogs find a bone. One saw it first; the other touched it first. Unable to decide who owns it, they bury it and go off to seek the opinion of others and in so doing almost lose the bone to another dog. The bold use of color adds spark and flair to the simple story.

HONORS

Skipper John's Cook Marcia Brown Illustrated by the author Scribner

Beans! That was the trouble. The Skipper's crew refuses to sign on until a cook is found who does not fix beans morning, noon, and night. Young Si is hired on. After he has fried his 259th fish, the crew wants to know what else he can cook. Beans! Illustrations capture the expressions of the crew—and of the pots and pans.

Bear Party William Pène du Bois Illustrated by the author Viking

When the koala bears become very angry with each other, it is "the wise old bear who lives at the top of the tallest Eucalyptus tree" who decides what to do. The koala bears are shown dressed in all the finery of a masked costume party, while wonderful onomatopoeic words describe the sounds of the musical instruments.

Mr. T. W. Anthony Woo Marie Hall Ets Illustrated by the author Viking

Pandemonium reigns at the cobbler's when his dog and cat fight each other, and then both chase Mr. T. W. Anthony Woo, the mouse. Sister and her parrot move in, and things go from bad to worse until the enemies band together to create peace. Illustrations are contained within borders and suggest the control the cobbler wishes he had.

Feather Mountain Elizabeth Olds Illustrated by the author Houghton

At one time all birds were naked and pink and featherless. One day they ask the Great Spirit to give them coverings. Black-and-white and color pictures depict the birds as they scurry around finding just the right colors to blend with their habitats.

All Falling Down Gene Zion Illustrated by Margaret Bloy Graham Harper

So many things fall—petals, rain, apples, even Daddy's book when his head begins to nod. This quiet, reflective book is illustrated with pastel colors. There is a surprise ending when Daddy tosses the baby in the air.

1951 AWARD

The Egg Tree   Katherine Milhous   Illustrated by the author   Scribner

An Easter morning egg hunt leads to the discovery of long forgotten decorated eggs. With them the family begins a new tradition. Pennsylvania Dutch folk designs border many of the pages; the colors found in hex signs dominate the paintings that interpret the story.

HONORS

Dick Whittington and His Cat   Marcia Brown
Illustrated by the author   Scribner

Artistic linoleum block cuts have humor and charm. They illustrate a simple retelling of the folktale of the boy who was made wealthy because he listened to his cat.

If I Ran the Zoo   Dr. Seuss, pseud. (Theodor Seuss Geisel)
Illustrated by the author   Random House

Young Gerald McGrew likes the zoo but knows that if he ran it he would make some changes. He imagines all kinds of fantastic beasts with wonderfully creative names and unusual shapes and habits. Zany, whimsical illustrations are perfect for the imaginative verse.

The Two Reds   Will, pseud. (William Lipkind)
Illustrated by Nicolas, pseud. (Nicolas Mordvinoff)   Harcourt Brace

Red, the boy, sets out to play at the same time Red, an independent cat, sets out for food. The sense of impending chaos mounts as each gets in trouble at the same time in different parts of town. Sparse line drawings with brilliant splashes of red add spark to the illustrations.

T-Bone, the Baby Sitter   Clare Turlay Newberry
Illustrated by the author   Harper

T-Bone the cat loves to sit. That is what makes him such a fine baby-sitter—until the day he awakens with a twinkle in his eye, full of mischief. Expressive illustrations show the baby's extreme displeasure when T-Bone is taken away to the country and his pleasure when he returns.

The Most Wonderful Doll in the World   Phyllis McGinley
Illustrated by Helen Stone   Lippincott

Duley loses a new doll. Her imagination runs wild as she describes the lost and most wonderful doll in the world as she wants it to be, not as it is. The book is decorated with four-color and black-and-white illustrations and borders.

1950 AWARD

Song of the Swallows   Leo Politi   Illustrated by the author   Scribner

The bell ringer and gardener of the mission church in Capistrano tells Juan the history of the mission churches and of the return of the swallows every St. Joseph's Day. Pinks, grays, yellows, and greens in muted tones convey friendship and a respect for nature. Two songs are included in the text.

HONORS

Henry—Fisherman   Marcia Brown   Illustrated by the author   Scribner

> To be a fisherman a boy has to be able to swim very fast in case a shark is near. As the day when Juan will be allowed on the fishing boat draws closer, sights and sounds of a childhood in the Virgin Islands are portrayed in brown, coral, yellow, and green.

The Wild Birthday Cake   Lavinia R. Davis
Illustrated by Hildegard Woodward   Doubleday

> Johnny is so excited about going on an adventurous hike that he almost forgets his friend's seventy-fifth birthday. On his hike he catches a wild duck and later gives it to his friend as a gift. Abundant on the pages are the yellows and greens of spring.

Bartholomew and the Oobleck
Dr. Seuss, pseud. (Theodor Seuss Geisel)   Illustrated by the author
Random House

> Tired of snow, fog, rain, and sunshine, the king wants something new to fall from the sky. What he gets are green, gooey globs of oobleck that threaten to destroy the kingdom. Comical illustrations in black-and-white become greener and greener as the oobleck spreads.

America's Ethan Allen   Stewart Holbrook   Illustrated by Lynd Ward   Houghton

> Brave and rebellious Ethan Allen is born in the wilds of the old colony of Connecticut. He grows into a rugged frontier hero who leads the Green Mountain Boys. The illustrations and writing style resound with patriotism and historical significance.

The Happy Day   Ruth Krauss   Illustrated by Marc Simont   Harper

> The woodland animals are all in their winter's sleep when something causes them to open their eyes and sniff. Suspense mounts as they all race toward the thing that has caused them to awaken. Black-and-white drawings portray joyous animals as they leap around a bright yellow flower—the first sign of spring and the only color in the book.

1949 AWARD

The Big Snow   Berta and Elmer Hader
Illustrated by the authors   Macmillan

When they see the wild geese flying overhead, all the woodland animals scurry to get ready for winter. After the big snow they slowly emerge to find food. Black-and-white drawings are occasionally interspersed with full-color paintings.

HONORS

Blueberries for Sal   Robert McCloskey   Illustrated by the author   Viking

On the same day that Little Sal and her mother go to Blueberry Hill to pick blueberries, so do Little Bear and his mother. Soon a mix-up in mothers occurs. Dark blue-and-white type and drawings promote gentle humor against the ruggedness of Blueberry Hill.

All around the Town   Phyllis McGinley   Illustrated by Helen Stone   Lippincott

Snappy rhythm of the text and splashes of color in the illustrations capture the gaiety and pace of city life. Each verse is about a city sight and the rhymes are arranged in alphabetical order, from Aeroplane to Zoo.

Juanita   Leo Politi   Illustrated by the author   Scribner

As Easter draws near, Juanita and her friends join in the parade for the Blessing of the Animals at the Old Mission Church. The text is lovingly illustrated and interspersed with some songs, making the warmth of a close-knit community in old Los Angeles come alive.

Fish in the Air   Kurt Wiese   Illustrated by the author   Viking

On their way to fly a great big kite, Fish and his kite are grabbed by a Tai Fung, or big wind. It sends them on a high-flying adventure. Colorful paintings portray the excitement caused when Fish flies over town and countryside.

1948 AWARD

White Snow, Bright Snow   Alvin Tresselt
Illustrated by Roger Duvoisin   Lothrop

Slowly the snow begins to fall and the adults busy themselves preparing for it. The children revel in it. A dark blue background gives way to white as the heavy snow melts and spring breaks forth. Reds and yellows provide a cheerful balance.

HONORS

Stone Soup: An Old Tale　Marcia Brown　Illustrated by the author　Scribner

> An inhospitable town refuses to help three hungry soldiers. When the soldiers decide to make a soup of stones, curiosity overcomes the peasants and they learn a lesson in cooperation. Orange and brown pictures portray peasant life in a long-ago French village.

Roger and the Fox　Lavinia R. Davis
Illustrated by Hildegard Woodward　Doubleday

> Roger wants to see the wild fox and tries many times before he figures out how to be quick and quiet enough to do it. The pictures turn from the warm hues of fall to the cold blues of winter before patience and ingenuity finally pay off.

McElligot's Pool　Dr. Seuss, pseud. (Theodor Seuss Geisel)
Illustrated by the author　Random House

> Told that he is some sort of fool for trying to catch fish in McElligot's pool, Marco visualizes the possibility that the pool is connected to the sea. Wonderfully imaginative creatures with fantastic names swim across the pages of this story told in verse.

Song of Robin Hood　Selected by Anne Malcolmson; Music by Grace Castagnetta
Designed and illustrated by Virginia Lee Burton　Houghton

> Eighteen ballads of Robin Hood, most traced back to their original tunes, are exuberantly presented in verse, music, and art. The five hundred verses are decorated in a style reminiscent of miniature drawings of the fifteenth century. Its words meant to be sung not read, the book provides an energetic and lyrical introduction to the famous Robin Hood.

Bambino the Clown　Georges Schreiber　Illustrated by the author　Viking

> The full colors and excitement of a circus clown's act are experienced by a sad young boy whom Bambino befriends. Peter is invited into the clown's dressing room, watches him apply his makeup, and becomes a very funny part of the show.

1947 AWARD

The Little Island　Golden MacDonald, pseud. (Margaret Wise Brown)　Illustrated by Leonard Weisgard　Doubleday

The seasons come and go and little by little the small island changes. One day a kitten visits the island and discovers that it does not stand alone but is connected underwater to land. The moods of the mostly green and blue drawings change with the seasons.

HONORS

The Boats on the River Marjorie Flack Illustrated by Jay Hyde Barnum Viking

There are warships, ocean liners, rowboats, and many other boats on the river that flows by the city and out to sea. Full-color paintings show close and distant views of the boats.

Timothy Turtle Al Graham Illustrated by Tony Palazzo Robert Welch

On the day Timothy flips over on his back, each animal tries to help him right himself. The wise frog tells the other animals that what they could not do as individuals they can do as a group. Action-packed drawings add tautness and humor to the tale.

Pedro, the Angel of Olvera Street Leo Politi Illustrated by the author Scribner

Young Pedro, who sings like an angel, leads La Posada, the Christmas procession, on Olvera Street in Los Angeles. For nine consecutive nights he wears red wings and sings carols of Christian pilgrims. The soft colors reflect the solemnity of the procession. Music is included.

Rain Drop Splash Alvin Tresselt Illustrated by Leonard Weisgard Lothrop

A single rain drop splashes down. Soon it is joined by others, and a puddle is formed. The puddle grows bigger and bigger until the rain drops at last become the sea, and the rain stops. The poetic patterns of the text and the drenched look of the pictures provide a closeness to nature.

Sing in Praise: A Collection of the Best Loved Hymns Stories and arrangements by Opal Wheeler Illustrated by Marjorie Torrey Dutton

Twenty-five perennially popular Christian hymns have been arranged to simple piano scores. Most of the hymns are accompanied by a laudatory story about how the particular words or melody came to be written. Romanticized illustrations show pious children looking heavenward.

1946 AWARD

The Rooster Crows: A Book of American Rhymes and Jingles
Maud and Miska Petersham Illustrated by the authors Macmillan

A potpourri of the rhymes, jingles, and chants of American children is treated to a variety of visual interpretations. Each rhyme is illustrated with humor and rhythm.

HONORS

Little Lost Lamb   Golden MacDonald, pseud. (Margaret Wise Brown)
Illustrated by Leonard Weisgard   Doubleday

> When the little black lamb strays from the rest of the flock, the little shepherd and his sheepdog go into the perilous night in search of it. The mood of the story changes from bright, frolicsome pictures of the frisky lamb to dark browns that reflect the concern the boy has for the lost animal.

My Mother Is the Most Beautiful Woman in the World   Becky Reyher
Illustrated by Ruth Chrisman Gannett   Lothrop

> When a little girl becomes lost, she describes her mother with her heart not with her eyes. Colorful pictures reflect the spirit of the old Russian proverb, "We do not love people because they are beautiful, but they seem beautiful to us because we love them."

Sing Mother Goose   Music by Opal Wheeler
Illustrated by Marjorie Torrey   Dutton

> Fifty-two of the most familiar Mother Goose nursery rhymes have been arranged to original, sprightly music. The piano scores and the rhymes are accompanied by illustrations of children, many of whom are in late-Victorian dress.

You Can Write Chinese   Kurt Wiese   Illustrated by the author   Viking

> In China in the 1940s, a classroom of boys receives a language lesson. The teacher explains that there are no letters in the Chinese language, only words based on ancient pictures. Most of the book consists of large drawings of Chinese characters superimposed on drawings of objects that represent the words.

1945 AWARD

Prayer for a Child   Rachel Field
Illustrated by Elizabeth Orton Jones   Macmillan

A child's bedtime prayer asks for blessings on things that are familiar to small children with such lines as, "Bless other children, far and near, And keep them safe and free from fear." Brief lines of the prayer are illustrated with full-page, reverent golden-toned drawings.

HONORS

In the Forest   Marie Hall Ets   Illustrated by the author   Viking

> With his new horn and paper hat a little boy takes a walk in the forest, and along the way he meets storks, kangaroos, bears, and other animals who join his parade.

All disappear when the boy's father comes hunting for him. There is a strong contrast between the white figures and the black forest backgrounds.

Yonie Wondernose   Marguerite de Angeli   Illustrated by the author   Doubleday

His father has promised him something very special as soon as seven-year-old Yonie learns to handle responsibilities like a man. Strongly depicted in the illustrations and the text is the hard but cheerful way of life on an Amish farm.

The Christmas Anna Angel   Ruth Sawyer   Illustrated by Kate Seredy   Viking

In a story set in Hungary during the war, Anna longs for a Christmas cake shaped like a little clock. The deprivations caused by the war contrast with the happy family traditions of Christmas. While heavy on text, the book has several illustrations reflective of the folk culture.

Mother Goose: Seventy-seven Verses   Illustrated by Tasha Tudor   Oxford

Seventy-seven Mother Goose rhymes are gathered together in this small book. Many of the rhymes are familiar, but some are those usually found only in complete works. Quaint, soft-colored pictures abound on every page.

1944 AWARD

Many Moons   James Thurber   Illustrated by Louis Slobodkin

Harcourt Brace

After eating too many raspberry tarts, the princess declares that if she can have the moon she will be well again. The wisdom of the royal advisors fails. The common sense of the jester prevails. Washes of pinks and blues complement the whimsy of the humorous fantasy.

HONORS

A Child's Good Night Book   Margaret Wise Brown
Illustrated by Jean Charlot   W. R. Scott

Night has come and everything is going to sleep. Animals, children, and even engines are sleepy. The brief story ends with a prayer to bless and guard "small things that have no words." The repetitious phrases and drawings are designed to bring on drowsiness.

The Good-Luck Horse   Chih-Yi Chan   Illustrated by Plato Chan   Whittlesey

A lonely boy in ancient China creates a very small paper horse that he can hold in his hand. Magically the horse becomes real. Although the magician names it "Good-Luck Horse," the story proves that sometimes good luck is bad luck and vice versa. The adventures of the horse are re-created in the line and wash drawings.

The Mighty Hunter   Berta and Elmer Hader
Illustrated by the authors   Macmillan

> Little Brave Heart's mother tells him to go to school so he can grow up to be a wise leader, but he goes hunting instead. Each animal in turn tells him that there is a better animal to shoot. The bear chastises him for hunting for "fun," and chases him to school. The illustrations alternate between black-and-white and desert colors.

Small Rain: Verses from the Bible   Chosen by Jessie Orton Jones
Illustrated by Elizabeth Orton Jones   Viking

> Brief Bible verses taken from the King James Version of the Old and New Testaments are illustrated with children doing everyday things—romping, playing, sitting quietly, sharing, running, crying, and sleeping. Each verse relates in some way to what the children are doing.

Pierre Pidgeon   Lee Kingman   Illustrated by Arnold Edwin Bare   Houghton

> Seven-year-old Pierre has long been fascinated by the boat-in-bottle in the shop. Finally he purchases it, and before he gets it home he breaks it. Studying the broken model, he succeeds in figuring out how the boat got into the bottle. Gray, green, and peach tones reflect a Canadian fishing village.

1943 AWARD

The Little House   Virginia Lee Burton
Illustrated by the author   Houghton

Built long ago far out in the country, the Little House is now surrounded by the city. Circular shapes abound in the illustrations and the lines of type. Bright, happy colors give way to dark, moody ones as progress overtakes the house. Light colors return when the house is moved to a new countryside.

HONORS

Dash and Dart   Mary and Conrad Buff   Illustrated by the authors   Viking

> In simple, poetic text and mood-capturing sepia paintings, the first year in the life of two fawns is described. A great reverence for nature is felt throughout the book.

Marshmallow   Clare Turlay Newberry   Illustrated by the author   Harper

> Oliver the cat lives a blissful life of eating and sleeping until the lady who takes care of him brings home a bundle of live, soft fur. Suddenly Oliver is terrified when he is confronted with a bunny named Marshmallow. The pictures show how their relationship grows until they both curl up together.

1942 AWARD

Make Way for Ducklings   Robert McCloskey
Illustrated by the author   Viking

Having hatched her ducklings and taught them to march nicely in single file, Mrs. Mallard decides to take them straight through Boston's busy streets to their new home in the Public Garden and pond. Sketchy brown drawings humorously show the ordeal the mallards face.

HONORS

In My Mother's House   Ann Nolan Clark
Illustrated by Velino Herrera   Viking

Daily life of the pueblo as seen through the eyes of the children is described in a rhythmic, simple prose. Many aspects of life—houses, food, clothing, and agriculture—are pictured. Tribal designs and pen-and-ink and color drawings depict the Tawa life.

Nothing at All   Wanda Gág   Illustrated by the author   Coward

Three orphan dogs, two visible and one invisible, are adopted by two children. It takes a jackdaw, some magic, and a lot of energetic work by Nothing At All to become Something After All. Intriguing, lightly colored lithographs show the invisible become visible.

Paddle-to-the-Sea   Holling Clancy Holling   Illustrated by the author   Houghton

In the Canadian wilderness, a young boy carves a canoe with an Indian figure seated in it, then launches it from Lake Nipigon. The text and illustrations are filled with information about the scenes the canoe passes, from the quiet byways, to a sawmill, to a raging forest fire.

An American ABC   Maud and Miska Petersham
Illustrated by the authors   Macmillan

Familiar symbols, historic places, and legendary figures form the basis of this patriotic interpretation of the alphabet. Decorated in red, white, blue, and black, each letter provides a brief lesson in American history. The strength and courage of those who shaped America are visible in the drawings.

1941 AWARD

They Were Strong and Good   Robert Lawson
Illustrated by the author   Viking

Writing of his mother and father and their mothers and fathers, Lawson says they, like the ancestors of many others, were never famous but were "strong and good" and helped to build America. Line-and-brush drawings are sometimes humorous but more often depict the strength and goodness of the land and its people.

HONOR

April's Kittens   Clare Turlay Newberry   Illustrated by the author   Harper

> After her cat has kittens, April must decide on the one cat to keep. Illustrations of the black cats make them look fuzzy and furry. Occasional touches of red add a dash of color.

1940 AWARD

Abraham Lincoln   Ingri and Edgar Parin d'Aulaire
Illustrated by the authors   Doubleday, Doran

Well-known anecdotes of Lincoln, particularly of his youth and prairie years, are recounted with strength and humor in this picture biography. Lithographs in color and black and white reveal details of American life in the 1800s.

HONORS

Madeline   Ludwig Bemelmans   Illustrated by the author   Simon & Schuster

> High-spirited Madeline may be the smallest of the twelve little girls at Miss Clavel's school, but she is by far the bravest. Lilting rhythmic text and simple, childlike paintings provide a tour of Paris and introduce a spunky heroine.

The Ageless Story   Lauren Ford   With its Antiphons pictured by the author
Dodd, Mead

> The story of the Christ Child is told through Gregorian music, biblical text, and illustrations that are an adaptation of illuminated manuscripts. The illustrations are a blend of early Renaissance religious art in a New England setting.

Cock-a-Doodle-Doo   Berta and Elmer Hader
Illustrated by the authors   Macmillan

> In a reversal of the story of the Ugly Duckling, a chick is hatched by a duck. The ducklings make fun of him, and soon the chick goes off in search of others like

him. In alternating color and black-and-white pictures he faces several perils before landing in the hen house.

1939 AWARD

Mei Li Thomas Handforth Illustrated by the author
Doubleday, Doran

The New Year Fair is in the city, and Mei Li's brother has been told that he can go, but little girls have to stay home. Strong, bold line drawings present many aspects of Chinese culture and customs as they follow the irrepressible Mei Li, who sneaks off for a grand time at the fair.

HONORS

The Forest Pool Laura Adams Armer Illustrated by the author
Longmans, Green

> Glowing with the bright golden colors of South America, stylized pictures show two boys as they go in search of the iguana in the bell-flower tree. The boys ponder the animals that know so much but never reveal their secrets.

Andy and the Lion James Daugherty Illustrated by the author Viking

> The old story of Androcles and the lion is retold in a modern setting. Andy signs out a book about lions from the library. The next day he comes upon a lion with a thorn stuck in his paw. Told and illustrated with robust tall-tale humor, the twists of the tale lead to a fine friendship.

Snow White and the Seven Dwarfs
Translated and illustrated by Wanda Gág Coward

> In this little book the Brothers Grimm story of the vain, wicked stepmother, the seven dwarfs, and the beautiful princess is retold with much repetition. The black-and-white drawings are filled with rounded shapes that continue the repetitiousness of the story.

Wee Gillis Munro Leaf Illustrated by Robert Lawson Viking

> The Highland relatives want Wee Gillis to stalk stags with them. The Lowland relatives want him to tend the cows. After years of doing both, Wee Gillis has powerful lungs from calling the cows, and he has learned to sit very still from stalking stags—just the skills needed to play a bagpipe! Line drawings sparkle with humorous spirit.

Barkis   Clare Turlay Newberry   Illustrated by the author   Harper

A bickering brother and sister squabble over the ownership of a new puppy and cat. They finally reach a solution that makes them both happy. Soft brown-and-black drawings of the winsome cat and dog are set against white backgrounds.

1938 AWARD

Animals of the Bible: A Picture Book   Text from the King James Bible selected by Helen Dean Fish   Illustrated by Dorothy P. Lathrop   Stokes

The Old and New Testaments of the King James Version are the sources for thirty-one stories about animals. Black-and-white full-page illustrations include the flora of biblical lands and portray the animals with reverence.

HONORS

Seven Simeons: A Russian Tale
Retold and illustrated by Boris Artzybasheff   Viking

King Douda, wise, rich, strong, and very handsome, decides to marry a princess as beautiful as himself. To help him in his quest, he engages seven brothers, each of whom has a special skill that, by the tale's end, is used in a most unusual manner. Love triumphs in the end in this whimsically decorated book with neat color line drawings.

Four and Twenty Blackbirds: Nursery Rhymes of Yesterday
Recalled for Children of Today   Collected by Helen Dean Fish
Illustrated by Robert Lawson   Stokes

The twenty-four nursery rhymes found here were culled from out-of-print books or "rescued from memories of older people." Most are long and filled with the jingling and sturdy humor of traditional nursery rhymes. They are illustrated with vigorous drawings in black and green. Simple music is given for those rhymes that have tunes.

The Media Used in Caldecott Picture Books
Notes toward a Definitive List

CHRISTINE BEHRMANN

Since 1938 more than one hundred artists have illustrated picture books that have won a Caldecott Award or been named Caldecott Honor Books. Each of these books has won the accolade because of the quality of its illustrator's distinctive style, a style that has evoked images and ideas in the reader's mind that remain long after the book is closed. As the book is reviewed and discussed, we talk much about the artist's imagination, talent, and unique eye. Mentioned less often is the physical process by which the images imagined by that unique eye come to life and the role of the artist's medium (paint, lithography, pen and ink, etc.) in that process. In the fifty years since the Caldecott Award was first given, there has apparently been no systematic attempt to list the media used to create the honored picture books. This is a loss, because it is scholarly information useful to the study of children's literature, and because it is a humbling and educating experience to see the care, skill, and sheer craftsmanship that go into the creation of a truly distinguished picture book. This article is an initial attempt to fill the void.

What follows must be a work in progress, as digging out this information is a process that involves not only library research, but also correspondence with the artist, editor, or art director, and with other collections. In some cases, the information may be lost forever because it was never written down in bibliographic descriptions, and the author and the publisher are no longer available to be questioned. It is heartening to note that some publishers, such as Dial and Greenwillow, are beginning to list—in

Reprinted, with changes, from *Journal of Youth Services in Libraries* (Winter 1988): 198–212. Christine Behrmann was Children's Materials Specialist, Office of Children's Services, New York Public Library.

the books themselves—the media used in creating the pictures. This practice will certainly aid in the appreciation of the picture book as art.

The data listed below are thus, in many cases, preliminary only. Guesses were not made. When hard data were not found, the entry was left blank, except for a question mark. No information was regarded as final unless it was found in two independent secondary sources (review, bibliography, catalog, etc.) or available from one primary source (book, artist, publisher, Caldecott citation). Information from only one secondary source was included but marked preliminary by a question mark in parentheses. Corrections and added information are earnestly solicited. The most important result is to obtain, eventually, a complete, accurate list.

Many deserve thanks for their kind cooperation thus far, but it is most important to single out Lyn Lacey, whose excellent idea this project was.

1938 / AWARD

Animals of the Bible: A Picture Book Text from the King James Bible selected by Helen Dean Fish; Illustrated by Dorothy P. Lathrop (Stokes)—black-and-white lithographs

HONORS

Seven Simeons: A Russian Tale Retold and illustrated by Boris Artzybasheff (Viking)—pen and ink

Four and Twenty Blackbirds: Nursery Rhymes of Yesterday Recalled for Children of Today Collected by Helen Dean Fish; Illustrated by Robert Lawson (Stokes)— drawings in pen and tempera

1939 / AWARD

Mei Li by Thomas Handforth; Illustrated by the author (Doubleday, Doran)—brush and lithograph pencil (?)

HONORS

The Forest Pool by Laura Adams Armer; Illustrated by the author (Longmans, Green)—medium not known

Andy and the Lion by James Daugherty; Illustrated by the author (Viking)—charcoal rubbed off on light gray transfer and rubbed in (?)

Snow White and the Seven Dwarfs Translated and illustrated by Wanda Gág (Coward)—lithographs (?)

Wee Gillis by Munro Leaf; Illustrated by Robert Lawson (Viking)—drawings in pen and tempera

Barkis by Clare Newberry; Illustrated by the author (Harper)—charcoal pencil and watercolor wash

1940 / AWARD

Abraham Lincoln by Ingri and Edgar Parin d'Aulaire; Illustrated by the authors (Doubleday, Doran)—lithographic pencil on stone

HONORS

Madeline by Ludwig Bemelmans; Illustrated by the author (Simon & Schuster)— brush, pen, and watercolor (?)

The Ageless Story by Lauren Ford; Illustrated by the author (Dodd, Mead)— painting; touches of gold leaf (?)

Cock-a-Doodle-Doo by Berta and Elmer Hader; Illustrated by the authors (Macmillan)—watercolor

1941 / AWARD

They Were Strong and Good by Robert Lawson; Illustrated by the author (Viking)— brush and ink

HONOR

April's Kittens by Clare Turlay Newberry; Illustrated by the author (Harper)—ink, charcoal, and watercolor

1942 / AWARD

Make Way for Ducklings by Robert McCloskey; Illustrated by the author (Viking)— lithographic crayon on stone

HONORS

In My Mother's House by Ann Nolan Clark; Illustrated by Velino Herrera (Viking)— medium not known

Nothing at All by Wanda Gág; Illustrated by the author (Coward)—original lithographs in color

Paddle-to-the-Sea by Holling Clancy Holling; Illustrated by the author (Houghton)—full-color oil paintings

An American ABC by Maud and Miska Petersham; Illustrated by the authors (Macmillan)—pencil and preseparated watercolor

1943 / AWARD

The Little House by Virginia Lee Burton; Illustrated by the author (Houghton)— watercolor

HONORS

Dash and Dart by Mary and Conrad Buff; Illustrated by the authors (Viking)—
lithographs (?)

Marshmallow by Clare Newberry; Illustrated by the author (Harper)—charcoal (?)

1944 / AWARD

Many Moons by James Thurber; Illustrated by Louis Slobodkin (Harcourt Brace)—
pen and ink; watercolor

HONORS

A Child's Good Night Book by Margaret Wise Brown; Illustrated by Jean Charlot
(W. R. Scott)—crayon drawings

The Good-Luck Horse by Chih-Yi Chan; Illustrated by Plato Chan (Whittlesey)—
pen and ink; wash (?)

The Mighty Hunter by Berta and Elmer Hader; Illustrated by the authors
(Macmillan)—watercolor

Small Rain: Verses from the Bible Chosen by Jessie Orton Jones; Illustrated by
Elizabeth Orton Jones (Viking)—medium not known

Pierre Pidgeon by Lee Kingman; Illustrated by Arnold Edwin Bare (Houghton)—
preseparated gouache and ink drawings

1945 / AWARD

Prayer for a Child by Rachel Field; Illustrated by Elizabeth Orton Jones
(Macmillan)—pen and ink; watercolor

HONORS

In the Forest by Marie Hall Ets; Illustrated by the author (Viking)—paper batik

Yonie Wondernose by Marguerite de Angeli; Illustrated by the author (Doubleday)—
color separations done in pen, ink, pencil, and watercolor

The Christmas Anna Angel by Ruth Sawyer; Illustrated by Kate Seredy (Viking)—
medium not known

Mother Goose and Seventy-seven Verses Illustrated by Tasha Tudor (Oxford)—
graphite and watercolor (?)

1946 / AWARD

The Rooster Crows: A Book of American Rhymes and Jingles by Maud and Miska
Petersham; Illustrated by the authors (Macmillan)—lithograph pencil with color
separations on acetate

HONORS

Little Lost Lamb by Golden MacDonald; Illustrated by Leonard Weisgard (Doubleday)—medium not known

My Mother Is the Most Beautiful Woman in the World by Becky Reyher; Illustrated by Ruth Chrisman Gannett (Lothrop)—original gouache and watercolor reproduced by four-match process using lithographic crayon

Sing Mother Goose by Opal Wheeler; Illustrated by Marjorie Torrey (Dutton)—medium not known

You Can Write Chinese by Kurt Wiese; Illustrated by the author (Viking)—ink and watercolor separations

1947 / AWARD

The Little Island by Golden MacDonald; Illustrated by Leonard Weisgard (Doubleday)—gouache

HONORS

The Boats on the River by Marjorie Flack; Illustrated by Jay Hyde Barnum (Viking)—medium not known

Timothy Turtle by Al Graham; Illustrated by Tony Palazzo (Robert Welch)—black-and-white pen and ink (?)

Pedro, the Angel of Olvera Street by Leo Politi; Illustrated by the author (Scribner)—medium not known

Rain Drop Splash by Alvin Tresselt; Illustrated by Leonard Weisgard (Lothrop)—three colors preseparated with india ink on acetate overlays

Sing in Praise: A Collection of Best Loved Hymns Stories and arrangements by Opal Wheeler; Illustrated by Marjorie Torrey (Dutton)—medium not known

1948 / AWARD

White Snow, Bright Snow by Alvin Tresselt; Illustrated by Roger Duvoisin (Lothrop)—acetate separations in india ink

HONORS

Stone Soup: An Old Tale by Marcia Brown; Illustrated by the author (Scribner)—ink and watercolor (?)

Roger and the Fox by Lavinia Davis; Illustrated by Hildegard Woodward (Doubleday)—ink (?)

McElligot's Pool by Dr. Seuss; Illustrated by the author (Random House)—pencil and watercolor

Song of Robin Hood Selected by Anne Malcolmson; Music by Grace Castagnetta; Illustrated by Virginia Lee Burton (Houghton)—scratchboard

Bambino the Clown by Georges Schreiber; Illustrated by the author (Viking)—medium not known

1949 / AWARD

The Big Snow by Berta and Elmer Hader; Illustrated by the authors (Macmillan)—watercolor

HONORS

Blueberries for Sal by Robert McCloskey; Illustrated by the author (Viking)—lithographs (?)

All around the Town by Phyllis McGinley; Illustrated by Helen Stone (Lippincott)—medium not known

Juanita by Leo Politi; Illustrated by the author (Scribner)—tempera (?)

Fish in the Air by Kurt Wiese; Illustrated by the author (Viking)—ink and watercolor

1950 / AWARD

Song of the Swallows by Leo Politi; Illustrated by the author (Scribner)—tempera

HONORS

Henry—Fisherman by Marcia Brown; Illustrated by the author (Scribner)—collage (?)

The Wild Birthday Cake by Lavinia Davis; Illustrated by Hildegard Woodward (Doubleday)—medium not known

Bartholomew and the Oobleck by Dr. Seuss; Illustrated by the author (Random House)—pencil, crayon, and watercolor

America's Ethan Allen by Stewart Holbrook; Illustrated by Lynd Ward (Houghton)—full-color gouache paintings

The Happy Day by Ruth Krauss; Illustrated by Marc Simont (Harper)—medium not known

1951 / AWARD

The Egg Tree by Katherine Milhous; Illustrated by the author (Scribner)—tempera

HONORS

Dick Whittington and His Cat by Marcia Brown; Illustrated by the author (Scribner)—linoleum cuts

If I Ran the Zoo by Dr. Seuss; Illustrated by the author (Random House)—pencil, ink, and watercolor

The Two Reds by William Lipkind; Illustrated by Nicolas Mordvinoff (Harcourt Brace)—acetate separations using pen, ink, and brush

T-Bone, the Baby Sitter by Clare Turlay Newberry; Illustrated by the author (Harper)—pen, ink, and charcoal (?)

The Most Wonderful Doll in the World by Phyllis McGinley; Illustrated by Helen Stone (Lippincott)—medium not known

1952 / AWARD

Finders Keepers by William Lipkind; Illustrated by Nicolas Mordvinoff (Harcourt Brace)—acetate color separations for line reproduction

HONORS

Skipper John's Cook by Marcia Brown; Illustrated by the author (Scribner)—medium not known

Bear Party by William Pène du Bois; Illustrated by the author (Viking)—medium not known

Mr. T. W. Anthony Woo by Marie Hall Ets; Illustrated by the author (Viking)—paper batik

Feather Mountain by Elizabeth Olds; Illustrated by the author (Houghton)—preseparated art and watercolor wash (four-color)

All Falling Down by Gene Zion; Illustrated by Margaret Bloy Graham (Harper)—medium not known

1953 / AWARD

The Biggest Bear by Lynd Ward; Illustrated by the author (Houghton)—opaque watercolor

HONORS

Ape in a Cape by Fritz Eichenberg; Illustrated by the author (Harcourt Brace)—woodcuts; acetate separations

Five Little Monkeys by Juliet Kepes; Illustrated by the author (Houghton)—preseparated ink and watercolor wash (four-color)

One Morning in Maine by Robert McCloskey; Illustrated by the author (Viking)—lithographs (?)

Puss in Boots by Charles Perrault; Translated and illustrated by Marcia Brown (Scribner)—woodcut and watercolor (?)

The Storm Book by Charlotte Zolotow; Illustrated by Margaret Bloy Graham (Harper)—medium not known

1954 / AWARD

Madeline's Rescue by Ludwig Bemelmans; Illustrated by the author (Viking)—brush, pen, and watercolor

HONORS

The Steadfast Tin Soldier by Hans Christian Andersen; Illustrated by Marcia Brown (Scribner)—medium not known

Green Eyes by Abe Birnbaum; Illustrated by the author (Capitol)—medium not known

A Very Special House by Ruth Krauss; Illustrated by Maurice Sendak (Harper)—medium not known

Journey Cake, Ho! by Ruth Sawyer; Illustrated by Robert McCloskey (Viking)—medium not known

When Will the World Be Mine? The Story of a Snowshoe Rabbit by Miriam Schlein; Illustrated by Jean Charlot (W. R. Scott)—lithographs (?)

1955 / AWARD

Cinderella by Charles Perrault; Translated and illustrated by Marcia Brown (Scribner)—gouache, crayon, watercolor, and ink

HONORS

Wheel on the Chimney by Margaret Wise Brown; Illustrated by Tibor Gergely (Lippincott)—gouache (?)

The Thanksgiving Story by Alice Dalgliesh; Illustrated by Helen Sewell (Scribner)—medium not known

Book of Nursery and Mother Goose Rhymes Illustrated by Marguerite de Angeli (Doubleday)—Sharp Wolf pencils and watercolor

1956 / AWARD

Frog Went A-Courtin' Retold by John Langstaff; Illustrated by Feodor Rojankovsky (Harcourt Brace)—brush, ink, and crayon on acetate separations

HONORS

Play with Me by Marie Hall Ets; Illustrated by the author (Viking)—graphite separations

Crow Boy by Taro Yashima; Illustrated by the author (Viking)—pencil and brush separations

1957 / AWARD

A Tree Is Nice by Janice May Udry; Illustrated by Marc Simont (Harper)—gouache over watercolor

HONORS

Gillespie and the Guards by Benjamin Elkin; Illustrated by James Daugherty (Viking)—charcoal rubbed off on light gray transfer and inked (?)

Lion by William Pène du Bois; Illustrated by the author (Viking)—pen and india ink; color preseparated on Dinobase with lithographic pencil

Mr. Penny's Race Horse by Marie Hall Ets; Illustrated by the author (Viking)—paper batik

Anatole by Eve Titus; Illustrated by Paul Galdone (McGraw-Hill)—pen and ink with gray wash over graphite with paper collage (?)

1 Is One by Tasha Tudor; Illustrated by the author (Oxford)—graphite and watercolor (?)

1958 / AWARD

Time of Wonder by Robert McCloskey; Illustrated by the author (Viking)—casein

HONORS

Fly High, Fly Low by Don Freeman; Illustrated by the author (Viking)—colored pencil accented by outlines in ink

Anatole and the Cat by Eve Titus; Illustrated by Paul Galdone (McGraw)—pen and ink with gray wash over graphite with paper collage (?)

1959 / AWARD

Chanticleer and the Fox by Geoffrey Chaucer; Adapted and illustrated by Barbara Cooney (Crowell)—preseparated art: black and white on scratchboard; colors on Dinobase

HONORS

The House That Jack Built/La Maison Que Jacques A Batie by Antonio Frasconi; Illustrated by the author (Harcourt Brace)—woodcuts

What Do You Say, Dear? by Sesyle Joslin; Illustrated by Maurice Sendak (Young Scott)—pen and ink with watercolor wash separations

Umbrella by Taro Yashima; Illustrated by the author (Viking)—watercolor; pencil and brush for direct separations

1960 / AWARD

Nine Days to Christmas by Marie Hall Ets and Aurora Labastida; Illustrated by Marie Hall Ets (Viking)—pencil on Dinobase

HONORS

Houses from the Sea by Alice E. Goudey; Illustrated by Adrienne Adams (Scribner)—watercolor (?)

The Moon Jumpers by Janice May Udry; Illustrated by Maurice Sendak (Harper & Row)—tempera

1961 / AWARD

Baboushka and the Three Kings Adapted from a Russian Folk Tale by Ruth Robbins; Illustrated by Nicolas Sidjakov (Parnassus)—tempera and felt-tip pen in four colors

HONOR

Inch by Inch by Leo Lionni; Illustrated by the author (Obolensky)—rice paper collage and crayon

1962 / AWARD

Once a Mouse . . . A Fable by Marcia Brown (Scribner)—woodcuts and watercolor

HONORS

The Day We Saw the Sun Come Up by Alice E. Goudey; Illustrated by Adrienne Adams (Scribner)—graphite and gray wash with white gouache separations

Little Bear's Visit by Else Holmelund Minarik; Illustrated by Maurice Sendak (Harper & Row)—pen and ink with wash separations

The Fox Went Out on a Chilly Night: An Old Song Illustrated by Peter Spier (Doubleday)—pen and ink and watercolor on blue boards

1963 / AWARD

The Snowy Day by Ezra Jack Keats; Illustrated by the author (Viking)—collage: papers, paints, and gum-eraser stamps

HONORS

The Sun Is a Golden Earring by Natalia M. Belting; Illustrated by Bernarda Bryson (Holt Rinehart & Winston)—pencil

Mr. Rabbit and the Lovely Present by Charlotte Zolotow; Illustrated by Maurice Sendak (Harper & Row)—watercolor

1964 / AWARD

Where the Wild Things Are by Maurice Sendak; Illustrated by the author (Harper & Row)—india ink line over full-color tempera

HONORS

Swimmy by Leo Lionni; Illustrated by the author (Pantheon)—watercolor, rubber stamping, and pencil

All in the Morning Early by Sorche Nic Leodhas; Illustrated by Evaline Ness (Holt Rinehart & Winston)—medium not known

Mother Goose and Nursery Rhymes Illustrated by Philip Reed (Atheneum)— engravings on wood

1965 / AWARD

May I Bring a Friend? by Beatrice Schenk de Regniers; Illustrated by Beni Montresor (Atheneum)—pen-and-ink drawings on board in black with solid overlays and screened overlays on acetate

HONORS

A Pocketful of Cricket by Rebecca Caudill; Illustrated by Evaline Ness (Holt Rinehart & Winston)—medium not known

The Wave Adapted by Margaret Hodges from Lafacdio Hearn's *Gleanings in Buddha-Fields*; Illustrated by Blair Lent (Houghton)—ink and cardboard cutouts

Rain Makes Applesauce by Julian Scheer; Illustrated by Marvin Bileck (Holiday House)—pencil and watercolors (?)

1966 / AWARD

Always Room for One More by Sorche Nic Leodhas; Illustrated by Nonny Hogrogian (Holt Rinehart & Winston)—three-color preseparated art using pen for black line and pastels and wash for color

HONORS

Just Me by Marie Hall Ets; Illustrated by the author (Viking)—paper batik

Tom Tit Tot Retold and illustrated by Evaline Ness (Holt)—woodcuts

Hide and Seek Fog by Alvin Tresselt; Illustrated by Roger Duvoisin (Lothrop)—full-color gouache

1967 / AWARD

Sam, Bangs & Moonshine by Evaline Ness; Illustrated by the author (Holt Rinehart & Wilson)—three-color preseparated art using Japanese pen and wash; printer's ink; roller; string

HONOR

One Wide River to Cross Adapted by Barbara Emberley; Illustrated by Ed Emberley (Prentice-Hall)—woodcuts

1968 / AWARD

Drummer Hoff Adapted by Barbara Emberley; Illustrated by Ed Emberley (Prentice)—woodcuts and ink

HONORS

Frederick by Leo Lionni; Illustrated by the author (Pantheon)—collage with mixed media

Seashore Story by Yashima; Illustrated by the author (Viking)—watercolor and pastel

The Emperor and the Kite by Jane Yolen; Illustrated by Ed Young (World)—paper cuts

1969 / AWARD

The Fool of the World and the Flying Ship: A Russian Tale Retold by Arthur Ransome; Illustrated by Uri Shulevitz (Farrar Straus Giroux)—pen and brush with black and colored inks

HONOR

Why the Sun and the Moon Live in the Sky by Elphinstone Dayrell; Illustrated by Blair Lent (Houghton)—preseparated pen and ink in three colors

1970 / AWARD

Sylvester and the Magic Pebble by William Steig; Illustrated by the author (Windmill/ Simon & Schuster)—watercolor

HONORS

Goggles! by Ezra Jack Keats; Illustrated by the author (Macmillan)—oil paint and collage

Alexander and the Wind-Up Mouse by Leo Lionni; Illustrated by the author (Pantheon)—collage

Pop Corn and Ma Goodness by Edna Mitchell Preston; Illustrated by Robert Andrew Parker (Viking)—watercolor

Thy Friend, Obadiah by Brinton Turkle; Illustrated by the author (Viking)— medium not known

The Judge: An Untrue Tale by Harve Zemach; Illustrated by Margot Zemach (Farrar Straus Giroux)—watercolor, pen and ink

1971 / AWARD

A Story a Story: An African Tale Retold and illustrated by Gail E. Haley (Atheneum)—woodcuts

HONORS

Frog and Toad Are Friends by Arnold Lobel; Illustrated by the author (Harper & Row)—pencil drawings in three colors

In the Night Kitchen by Maurice Sendak; Illustrated by the author (Harper & Row)—line drawings and wash

The Angry Moon by William Sleator; Illustrated by Blair Lent (Atlantic/Little, Brown)—pen-and-ink drawings with acrylic glazes; full-color paintings

1972 / AWARD

One Fine Day Retold and illustrated by Nonny Hogrogian (Macmillan)—acrylic paintings with turpentine on gesso panels

HONORS

If All the Seas Were One Sea by Janina Domanska; Illustrated by the author (Macmillan)—etchings on zinc plates with brush-and-ink overlays

Moja Means One: Swahili Counting Book by Muriel Feelings; Illustrated by Tom Feelings (Dial)—graphite and paper collage

Hildilid's Night by Cheli Durán Ryan; Illustrated byArnold Lobel (Macmillan)—pen-and-ink drawings with yellow overlays

1973 / AWARD

The Funny Little Woman by Arlene Mosel; Illustrated by Blair Lent (Dutton)—pen-and-ink line drawings with full-color acrylic glazes; full-color paintings

HONORS

Hosie's Alphabet by Hosea, Tobias, and Lisa Baskin; Illustrated by Leonard Baskin (Viking)—watercolor

When Clay Sings by Byrd Baylor; Illustrated by Tom Bahti (Scribner)—medium not known

Snow White and the Seven Dwarfs: A Tale from the Brothers Grimm Translated by Randall Jarrell; Illustrated by Nancy Ekholm Burkert (Farrar Straus Giroux)—brush and colored inks

Anansi the Spider: A Tale from Ashanti Adapted and illustrated by Gerald McDermott (Holt Rinehart & Winston)—artwork preseparated in four colors with outline in ink

1974 / AWARD

Duffy and the Devil: A Cornish Tale Retold by Harve Zemach; Illustrated by Margot Zemach (Farrar Straus Giroux)—pen-and-ink drawings with watercolor

HONORS

Three Jovial Huntsmen Adapted and illustrated by Susan Jeffers (Bradbury)—pen-and-ink drawings with wash overlays painted in oils

Cathedral: The Story of Its Construction by David Macaulay; Illustrated by the author (Houghton)—pen and ink

1975 / AWARD

Arrow to the Sun: A Pueblo Indian Tale Adapted and illustrated by Gerald McDermott (Viking)—gouache and ink; black line preseparated

HONOR

Jambo Means Hello: Swahili Alphabet Book by Muriel Feelings; Illustrated by Tom Feelings (Dial)—graphite and paper collage

1976 / AWARD

Why Mosquitoes Buzz in People's Ears: A West African Tale by Verna Aardema; Illustrated by Leo and Diane Dillon (Dial)—india ink; watercolor; pastels; vellum and frisket masks

HONORS

The Desert Is Theirs by Byrd Baylor; Illustrated by Peter Parnall (Scribner)—pen and ink (?)

Strega Nona: An Old Tale Retold and illustrated by Tomie dePaola (Prentice-Hall)— watercolor and felt-tip pen over graphite

1977 / AWARD

Ashanti to Zulu: African Traditions by Margaret Musgrove; Illustrated by Leo and Diane Dillon (Dial)—pastels, watercolors, and acrylics

HONORS

Hawk, I'm Your Brother by Byrd Baylor; Illustrated by Peter Parnall (Scribner)—pen and ink (?)

Fish for Supper by M. B. Goffstein; Illustrated by the author (Dial)—ink drawings

The Contest Retold and illustrated by Nonny Hogrogian (Greenwillow/Morrow)— colored pencils and crayons for full color; pencil drawings for black and white

The Amazing Bone by William Steig; Illustrated by the author (Farrar Straus Giroux)—watercolor (?)

The Golem by Beverly Brodsky McDermott; Illustrated by the author (Lippincott)— gouache, watercolor, dye, and ink

1978 / AWARD

Noah's Ark by Peter Spier; Illustrated by the author (Doubleday)—F pencil on paper; watercolor and white pencil; negatives scratched

HONORS

Castle by David Macaulay; Illustrated by the author (Houghton)—pen and ink

It Could Always Be Worse: A Yiddish Folktale Retold and illustrated by Margot Zemach (Farrar Straus Giroux)—watercolor (?)

1979 / AWARD

The Girl Who Loved Wild Horses by Paul Goble; Illustrated by the author (Bradbury)—full-color pen and ink and watercolor

HONORS

Freight Train by Donald Crews; Illustrated by the author (Greenwillow/Morrow)—preseparated art; airbrush with transparent dyes

The Way to Start a Day by Byrd Baylor; Illustrated by Peter Parnall (Scribner)—pen and ink (?)

1980 / AWARD

Ox-Cart Man by Donald Hall; Illustrated by Barbara Cooney (Viking)—acrylics on gesso-coated board

HONORS

Ben's Trumpet by Rachel Isadora; Illustrated by the author (Greenwillow/Morrow)—pen and ink

The Treasure by Uri Shulevitz; Illustrated by the author (Farrar Straus Giroux)—watercolor with black line on acetate

The Garden of Abdul Gasazi by Chris Van Allsburg; Illustrated by the author (Houghton)—carbon pencil on Strathmore paper

1981 / AWARD

Fables by Arnold Lobel; Illustrated by the author (Harper & Row)—gouache and pencil

HONORS

The Grey Lady and the Strawberry Snatcher by Molly Bang; Illustrated by the author (Four Winds)—watercolor, sometimes with white gouache undercoat on gray construction paper

Mice Twice by Joseph Low; Illustrated by the author (Margaret K. McElderry/ Atheneum)—watercolor and pen and ink (?)

Truck by Donald Crews; Illustrated by the author (Greenwillow)—four halftone separations with black line drawings

The Bremen-Town Musicians Retold and illustrated by Ilse Plume (Doubleday)—colored pencil and graphite (?)

1982 / AWARD

Jumanji by Chris Van Allsburg; Illustrated by the author (Houghton)—conté pencil with conté dust

HONORS

Where the Buffaloes Begin by Olaf Baker; Drawings by Stephen Gammell (Warne)—pencil drawings (?)

On Market Street by Arnold Lobel; Illustrated by Anita Lobel (Greenwillow)—watercolor and pen and ink

Outside over There by Maurice Sendak; Illustrated by the author (Harper & Row)—medium not known

A Visit to William Blake's Inn by Nancy Willard; Illustrated by Alice and Martin Provensen (Harcourt Brace Jovanovich)—medium not known

1983 / AWARD

Shadow by Blaise Cendrars; Translated and illustrated by Marcia Brown (Scribner)—collage: paper, woodcuts, acrylics

HONORS

A Chair for My Mother by Vera Williams; Illustrated by the author (Greenwillow)—watercolor

When I Was Young in the Mountains by Cynthia Rylant; Illustrated by Diane Goode (Dutton)—watercolor and fine-colored pencil

1984 / AWARD

The Glorious Flight: Across the Channel with Louis Blériot, July 25, 1909 by Alice and Martin Provensen; Illustrated by the authors (Viking)—acrylic and pen and ink

HONORS

Ten, Nine, Eight by Molly Bang; Illustrated by the author (Greenwillow)—gouache (poster paint)

Little Red Riding Hood; Retold and illustrated by Trina Schart Hyman (Holiday House)—ink and acrylic (?)

1985 / AWARD

Saint George and the Dragon: A Golden Legend Adapted from Edmund Spenser's *Faerie Queen* by Margaret Hodges; Illustrated by Trina Schart Hyman (Little, Brown)—india ink and acrylic

HONORS

Hansel and Gretel Retold by Rika Lesser; Illustrated by Paul O. Zelinsky (Dodd, Mead)—oil paintings

The Story of Jumping Mouse; Retold and illustrated by John Steptoe (Lothrop)— graphite pencil and india ink on paper

Have You Seen My Duckling? by Nancy Tafuri; Illustrated by the author (Greenwillow)—watercolors and pastels

1986 / AWARD

The Polar Express by Chris Van Allsburg; Illustrated by the author (Houghton)— full-color oil pastel on pastel paper

HONORS

The Relatives Came by Cynthia Rylant; Illustrated by Stephen Gammell (Bradbury)—graphite and colored pencil

King Bidgood's in the Bathtub by Audrey Wood; Illustrated by Don Wood (Harcourt)—oil on pressed wood (?)

1987 / AWARD

Hey, Al by Arthur Yorinks; Illustrated by Richard Egielski (Farrar Straus Giroux)—watercolor

HONORS

The Village of Round and Square Houses by Ann Grifalconi; Illustrated by the author (Little, Brown)—pastels (?)

Alphabatics by Suse MacDonald; Illustrated by the author (Bradbury)—cells, vinyl acrylic; gouache

Rumpelstiltskin: From the German of the Brothers Grimm Retold and illustrated by Paul O. Zelinsky (Dutton)—oil paintings

1988 / AWARD

Owl Moon by Jane Yolen; Illustrated by John Schoenherr (Philomel)—pen and ink and watercolor

HONOR

Mufaro's Beautiful Daughters: An African Tale by John Steptoe; Illustrated by the author (Lothrop)—crosshatched pen and ink and watercolor

1989 / AWARD

Song and Dance Man by Karen Ackerman; Illustrated by Stephen Gammell (Knopf)—line drawings in colored pencil

HONORS

Mirandy and Brother Wind by Patricia C. McKissack; Illustrated by Jerry Pinkney (Knopf)—pencil and watercolor

Goldilocks and the Three Bears Retold and illustrated by James Marshall (Dial)—pen and ink and watercolor

The Boy of the Three-Year Nap by Dianne Snyder; Illustrated by Allen Say (Houghton)—brush-line, pen and ink, and watercolor

Free Fall by David Wiesner (Lothrop)—watercolor

1990 / AWARD

Lon Po Po by Ed Young; Translated and illustrated by the author (Philomel)—watercolor and pastels

HONORS

Color Zoo by Lois Ehlert; Illustrated by the author (Lippincott)—paper collage and die-cut forms

Hershel and the Hanukkah Goblins by Eric Kimmel; Illustrated by Trina Schart Hyman (Holiday House)—india ink and acrylic paint

Bill Peet: An Autobiography by Bill Peet; Illustrated by the author (Houghton)—pencil

The Talking Eggs by Robert San Souci; Illustrated by Jerry Pinkney (Dial)—pencil, colored-pencil, and watercolor

1991 / AWARD

Black and White by David Macaulay; Illustrated by the author (Houghton) "Seeing Things"—watercolor; "Problem Parents"—ink line and wash; "A Waiting Game"—watercolor and gouache; "Udder Confusion"—gouache paint

HONORS

Puss in Boots by Charles Perrault; Translated by Malcolm Arthur; Illustrated by Fred Marcellino (di Capua/Farrar Straus Giroux)—colored pencil on taupe textured illustration paper

"More, More, More," Said the Baby: 3 Love Stories by Vera B. Williams (Greenwillow)—gouache paints; lettering painted in watercolor based on Gill Sans Extra Bold Print

1992 / AWARD

Tuesday by David Wiesner; Illustrated by the author (Clarion)—watercolor

HONOR

Tar Beach by Faith Ringgold; Illustrated by the author (Crown)—acrylic on canvas

1993 / AWARD

Mirette on the High Wire by Emily Arnold McCully; Illustrated by the author (Putnam)—watercolor

HONORS

The Stinky Cheese Man & Other Fairly Stupid Tales by Jon Scieszka; Illustrated by Lane Smith (Viking)—oil and mixed media

Working Cotton by Sherley Anne Williams; Illustrated by Carole Byard (Harcourt Brace Jovanovich)—acrylic on Stonehenge white paper

Seven Blind Mice by Ed Young; Illustrated by the author (Philomel)—paper collage

1994 / AWARD

Grandfather's Journey by Allen Say; Illustrated by the author (Houghton)—watercolor

HONORS

Peppe the Lamplighter by Elisa Bartone; Illustrated by Ted Lewin (Lothrop)—watercolor

In the Small, Small Pond by Denise Fleming; Illustrated by the author (Henry Holt)—colored cotton pulp poured through hand-cut stencils

Owen by Kevin Henkes; Illustrated by the author (Greenwillow)—watercolor paints and black ink

Raven: A Trickster Tale from the Pacific Northwest by Gerald McDermott; Illustrated by the author (Harcourt Brace Jovanovich)—gouache, colored pencil, and pastel on heavyweight, cold-press watercolor paper

Yo! Yes? by Chris Raschka; Illustrated by the author (Orchard)—watercolor and charcoal pencil

1995 / AWARD

Smoky Night by Eve Bunting; Illustrated by David Diaz (Harcourt Brace)—acrylic paintings set against mixed media collage backgrounds

HONORS

Swamp Angel by Anne Isaacs; Illustrated by Paul O. Zelinsky (Dutton)—oil on cherry, maple, and birch veneers

John Henry by Julius Lester; Illustrated by Jerry Pinkney (Dial)—pencil, colored pencil, and watercolor

Time Flies by Eric Rohmann; Illustrated by the author (Crown)—oil

1996 / AWARD

Officer Buckle and Gloria by Peggy Rathmann; Illustrated by the author (Putnam)—watercolor and ink

HONORS

Alphabet City by Stephen T. Johnson; Illustrated by the author (Viking)—pastels, watercolors, gouache, and charcoal on hot pressed watercolor paper

Zin! Zin! Zin! a Violin by Lloyd Moss; Illustrated by Marjorie Priceman (Simon & Schuster)—gouache

The Faithful Friend by Robert D. San Souci; Illustrated by Brian Pinkney (Simon & Schuster)—scratchboard and oil

Tops & Bottoms Adapted and illustrated by Janet Stevens (Harcourt Brace)—watercolor, colored pencil, and gesso on paper made by hand by Ray Tomasso, Denver, Colorado

1997 / AWARD

Golem by David Wisniewski; Illustrated by the author (Clarion)—color-aid, coral, and bark cut papers

HONORS

Hush! A Thai Lullaby by Minfong Ho; Illustrated by Holly Meade (Orchard)—cut-paper collage with ink

The Graphic Alphabet by David Pelletier; Illustrated by the author (Orchard)—computer-generated images reproduced in full color

The Paperboy by Dav Pilkey; Illustrated by the author (Orchard)—acrylics and india ink

Starry Messenger: A Book Depicting the Life of a Famous Scientist, Mathematician, Astronomer, Philosopher, Physicist, Galileo Galilei by Peter Sís; Illustrated by the author (Farrar Straus Giroux)—pen and brown ink and watercolor

1998 / AWARD

Rapunzel by Paul O. Zelinsky; Illustrated by the author (Dutton)—oil reproduced in full color

HONORS

The Gardener by Sarah Stewart; Illustrated by David Small (Farrar Straus Giroux)—watercolor, ink pen line, and crayon

Harlem: A Poem by Walter Dean Myers; Illustrated by Christopher Myers (Scholastic)—ink, gouache, and cut-paper collage

There Was an Old Lady Who Swallowed a Fly by Simms Taback; Illustrated by the author (Viking)—mixed media and collage on kraft paper in color

1999 / AWARD

Snowflake Bentley by Jacqueline Briggs Martin; Illustrated by Mary Azarian
(Houghton)—woodcuts, hand-tinted with watercolors

HONORS

Duke Ellington by Andrea Davis Pinkney; Illustrated by Brian Pinkney
(Hyperion)—scratchboard renderings with gouache, luma dyes, and oil paint

No, David! by David Shannon; Illustrated by the author (Blue Sky/Scholastic)—
acrylics and colored pencil

Snow by Uri Shulevitz; Illustrated by the author (Farrar Straus Giroux)—ink and
watercolor washes

Tibet: Through the Red Box by Peter Sís; Illustrated by the author (Frances Foster
Farrar Straus Giroux)—watercolor, pen and ink, and oil pastel

2000 / AWARD

Joseph Had a Little Overcoat by Simms Taback; Illustrated by the author (Viking)—
watercolor, gouache, pencil, ink, and collage

HONORS

A Child's Calendar: Poems by John Updike; Illustrated by Trina Schart Hyman
(Holiday House)—pen and ink and watercolor

Sector 7 by David Wiesner; Illustrated by the author (Clarion)—watercolor

When Sofie Gets Angry—Really, Really Angry . . . by Molly Bang; Illustrated by the
author (Blue Sky/Scholastic)—gouache

The Ugly Duckling Adapted and illustrated by Jerry Pinkney (Morrow)—watercolor

2001 / AWARD

So You Want to Be President? by Judith St. George; Illustrated by David Small
(Philomel)—watercolor, ink, and pastel chalk

HONORS

Casey at the Bat: A Ballad of the Republic Sung in the Year 1888 by Ernest L. Thayer;
Illustrated by Christopher Bing (Handprint)—pen and ink scratchboard
engravings

Click, Clack, Moo: Cows That Type by Doreen Cronin; Illustrated by Betsy Lewin (Simon & Schuster)—watercolor

Olivia by Ian Falconer; Illustrated by the author (Anne Schwartz/Atheneum)—charcoal and gouache

2002 / AWARD

The Three Pigs by David Wiesner; Illustrated by the author (Clarion)—watercolor, gouache, colored inks, pencil, and colored pencil on Fabriano hot press paper

HONORS

Martin's Big Words: The Life of Dr. Martin Luther King, Jr. by Doreen Rappaport; Illustrated by Bryan Collier (Jump at the Sun/Hyperion)—watercolor, cut-paper collage

The Dinosaurs of Waterhouse Hawkins: An Illuminating History of Mr. Waterhouse Hawkins, Artist and Lecturer by Barbara Kerley; Illustrated by Brian Selznick (Scholastic)—acrylics

The Stray Dog: From a True Story by Reike Sassa by Marc Simont; Illustrated by the author (HarperCollins)—watercolor, gouache

2003 / AWARD

My Friend Rabbit by Eric Rohmann; Illustrated by the author (Roaring Brook)—hand-colored relief prints (watercolors)

HONORS

The Spider and the Fly by Mary Howitt; Illustrated by Tony DiTerlizzi (Simon & Schuster)—lamp black and titanium white holbein Acryla gouache and Berol Prismacolor pencil on Strathmore 5-ply, plate Bristol board and reproduced in silver and black duotone, graphite, and Adobe Photoshop

Hondo & Fabian by Peter McCarty; Illustrated by the author (Henry Holt)—pencil on watercolor paper

Noah's Ark by Jerry Pinkney; Illustrated by the author (SeaStar)—pencil, colored pencil, watercolors

2004 / AWARD

The Man Who Walked between the Towers by Mordicai Gerstein; Illustrated by the author (Roaring Brook)—pen and ink and oil paint on paper

HONORS

Ella Sarah Gets Dressed by Margaret Chodos-Irvine; Illustrated by the author (Harcourt)—various printmaking techniques on Rives paper

What Do You Do with a Tail like This? by Steve Jenkins and Robin Page; Illustrated by the authors (Houghton)—cut-paper collage

Don't Let the Pigeon Drive the Bus! by Mo Willems; Illustrated by the author (Hyperion)—Calligraphic cartoon drawings in dark marking pencil; scanned, cleaned, and colored in Photoshop

2005 / AWARD

Kitten's First Full Moon by Kevin Henkes; Illustrated by the author (Greenwillow)—gouache and colored pencil

HONORS

The Red Book by Barbara Lehman; Illustrated by the author (Houghton)—watercolor, gouache, and ink

Coming on Home Soon by Jacqueline Woodson; Illustrated by E. B. Lewis (Putnam)—watercolor on Arches paper

Knuffle Bunny: A Cautionary Tale by Mo Willems; Illustrated by the author (Hyperion)—hand-drawn ink sketches and digital photography—combined using a computer, which was also used to color and shade the sketches and give the photographs a sepia tone

2006 / AWARD

The Hello, Goodbye Window by Norton Juster; Illustrated by Chris Raschka (Michael di Capua Books)—watercolor, pastel crayons, charcoal pencil

HONORS

Rosa by Nikki Giovanni; Illustrated by Bryan Collier (Henry Holt)—watercolor, collage

Zen Shorts by Jon J. Muth; Illustrated by the author (Scholastic)—watercolor and ink

Hot Air: The (Mostly) True Story of the First Hot-Air Balloon Ride by Marjorie Priceman; Illustrated by the author (Anne Schwartz / Atheneum)—gouache and india ink on watercolor paper

Song of the Water Boatman and Other Pond Poems by Joyce Sidman; Illustrated by Beckie Prange (Houghton)—woodblock hand-colored with watercolor

2007 / AWARD

Flotsam by David Wiesner; Illustrated by the author (Clarion)—watercolor

HONORS

Gone Wild: An Endangered Animal Alphabet by David McLimans; Illustrated by the author (Walker)—pencil, pen, brush, india ink, bristol board, and computer

Moses: When Harriet Tubman Led Her People to Freedom by Carole Boston Weatherford; Illustrated by Kadir Nelson (Hyperion/Jump at the Sun)—oil and watercolor paints applied over pencil drawings on paper

SOME USEFUL DEFINITIONS

Acetate—a clear, plastic film used for overlays.

Airbrush—a mechanical painting tool that emits a fine spray of liquid or ink.

Batik—a wax-resistant process in which the design or image is first painted on the surface in wax so that, when the surface is dyed, the wax sections will not take the color.

Binder—the ingredient of a paint that holds together the particles of pigment and fixes them into a continuous film as the paint dries.

Color preseparation—the process by which an artist prepares, manually, the art to be printed in a four-, three-, or two-color book. This is done by preparing a master preseparation and overlays, each specifying a color to be reproduced for the image(s) contained in the area of the picture. When all of the overlays are printed together, the colors form the final picture.

Conté pencil—square-sectioned drawing chalks in black, white, sanguine, and sepia.

Dinobase—acetate sand-blasted to roughen the surface, making it similar to a lithographic stone; no longer used.

Dye—a coloring agent soluble in liquid that imparts color to a surface by being absorbed.

Engraving—any process by which a linear design is made on the surface of a hard and durable substance.

F pencil—a medium-hard graphite pencil.

Four-color process—a printing process in which the full range of the colors of an image is reproduced by means of four separate printing plates (black, blue, red, and yellow), which can be separated via camera, computer, or artist. After the separations, the plates are printed one on top of another in transparent process inks, as dictated by the separations, to create the final picture.

Frisket mask—a thin paper placed over an area not to be colored during painting or airbrushing.

Gouache—a method of painting with opaque colors.

Graphite—a carbon in stick form used for drawing.

India ink—a permanent black ink made of lampblack and glue binder.

Linoleum cuts—a relief printing process in which the image or design is cut into the surface of a block of linoleum.

Lithograph—a print made by drawing on limestone or a zinc plate with a greasy material, then wetting the plate and applying greasy ink that will only adhere to the drawn line. Dampened paper is then rubbed over the stone with a special press to create the final print. A lithographic crayon or pencil is often used for drawing on the lithographic stone, which is a block of limestone with its surface ground so an image can be made upon it. In offset lithography, the image is first transferred to an intermediate surface (a rubber blanket) before it is transferred to the paper.

Overlay—a transparent or translucent film attached to artwork carrying additional detail to be reproduced.

Paint—a substance consisting of a pigment evenly dispersed in a liquid which, when applied to a surface as a fluid, dries into a continuous film of color. In acrylic paint, the pigment is dispersed in an emulsion binder that is a liquid form of acrylic resin. In oil paint, the pigment is dispersed in a drying oil (usually linseed). In watercolor, the finely ground pigment is dispersed in a water-soluble gum binder and is transparent; gouache is a watercolor that uses opaque rather than transparent colors; tempera is an opaque watercolor paint in which the pigment is ground in water and mixed with egg yolk; it can also be poster paint.

Pastels—a drawing medium consisting of pigment mixed with gum binder, rolled or compressed into stick form.

Pigment—a finely ground colored powder that may be mixed with a liquid vehicle to make paint.

Scratchboard—an ink technique in which a white board is covered with india ink and a design or image is scratched into it.

Wash—an application of ink or watercolor heavily diluted with water to form a thin film of transparent color.

Woodcut—a relief printing process in which the image or design is cut into the surface of a plank-grain wood block.

BIBLIOGRAPHY

Children's Books: 1955–1957. New York: American Institute of Graphic Arts, 1958.

Children's Books: 1958–1960. New York: American Institute of Graphic Arts, 1960.

Children's Books: 1961–1962. New York: American Institute of Graphic Arts, 1962.

Cianciolo, Patricia J., ed. *Picture Books for Children.* 4th ed. American Library Assn., 1997.

de Angeli, Marguerite. *Butter at the Old Price.* Garden City: Doubleday, 1971.

Illustrations for Children: The Gladys English Collection. Sacramento: California Library Assn., Gladys English Memorial Collection Committee, 1963.

Jones, Helen. *Robert Lawson, Illustrator.* Boston: Little, 1972.

Kingman, Lee, and others. *Illustrators of Children's Books, 1957–1966.* Boston: Horn Book, 1968.

Kingman, Lee, ed. *Newbery and Caldecott Medal Books: 1956–1965.* Boston: Horn Book, 1965.

Kingman, Lee, ed. *Newbery and Caldecott Medal Books: 1966–1975.* Boston: Horn Book, 1975.

Kingman, Lee, ed. *Newbery and Caldecott Medal Books: 1976–1985.* Boston: Horn Book, 1986.

Lanes, Selma G. *The Art of Maurice Sendak.* New York: Abrams, 1980.

Larkin, David, ed. *The Art of Nancy Ekholm Burkert.* New York: Harper, 1977.

Lucie-Smith, Edward. *The Thames and Hudson Dictionary of Art Terms.* London: Thames & Hudson, 1984.

Martin, Judy. *The Longman Dictionary of Art.* Harlow, Eng.: Longman Group, 1986.

Miller, Bertha Mahony, and others. *Caldecott Medal Books: 1938–1957.* Boston: Horn Book, 1957.

Quick, John. *Artists' and Illustrators' Encyclopedia,* II ed. New York: McGraw-Hill, 1977.

Shulevitz, Uri. *Writing with Pictures.* New York: Watson-Guptill, 1985.

Viguers, Ruth Hill, and others. *Illustrators of Children's Books, 1946–1956.* Boston: Horn Book, 1958.

Also consulted: all issues of *Horn Book Magazine: 1938–1986.*

AUTHOR/ILLUSTRATOR INDEX

TITLE INDEX